The Way
Mum
Made It

The Way Mum Made It

Treasured family recipes
from Australian kitchens

*175 recipes shared by the
Over60 online community*

Edited by Alexandra O'Brien

ABC
Books

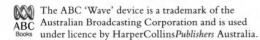 The ABC 'Wave' device is a trademark of the Australian Broadcasting Corporation and is used under licence by HarperCollins*Publishers* Australia.

First published in 2016
by HarperCollins*Publishers* Australia Pty Limited
ABN 36 009 913 517
harpercollins.com.au

HarperCollins*Publishers*
Level 13, 201 Elizabeth Street, Sydney, NSW 2000, Australia
Unit D1, 63 Apollo Drive, Rosedale, Auckland 0632, New Zealand
A 53, Sector 57, Noida, UP, India
1 London Bridge Street, London SE1 9GF, United Kingdom
2 Bloor Street East, 20th floor, Toronto, Ontario M4W 1A8, Canada
195 Broadway, New York, NY 10007, USA

National Library of Australia Cataloguing-in-Publication data:

The way mum made it: treasured family recipes from Australian kitchens /
edited by Alexandra O'Brien.
  978 0 7333 3503 7 (paperback)
  978 1 4607 0639 8 (ebook)
  Includes index.
  Cooking, Australian.
  Recipes.
  O'Brien, Alexandra, editor.
641.5994

Cover and internal design by Hazel Lam, HarperCollins Design Studio
Cover and internal images by shutterstock.com
Author photograph courtesy of Alexandra O'Brien
Printed and bound in Australia by Griffin Press
The papers used by HarperCollins in the manufacture of this book are a natural, recyclable product made from wood grown in sustainable plantation forests. The fibre source and manufacturing processes meet recognised international environmental standards, and carry certification.

Contents

Introduction

'Food and wine and friendship matter more than almost anything I can think of. Together they involve skill and craft and patience, and understanding of difference, and appreciation, and the desire to bring happiness to others.'
— Stephanie Alexander

As the famed Australian chef Stephanie Alexander points out, the power of food knows no bounds. Food and, more specifically, recipes transcend time. Recipes are passed down for generations, weaving the past with the present, enabling memories, skills, tradition and, perhaps most importantly, love to be carried through time. And more than that, food brings people together across age, culture and income — it is the one language that everyone in the world speaks.

This 'language' we talk of is first learnt in the home with family and loved ones. Whether it's becoming particularly fond of your mother's famous roast, learning to make your grandmother's apple pie, spending a day in the kitchen with your aunt preparing a Christmas feast, catching a fish and cooking it with your dad, or simply gathering around to share a meal, cooking is part of the fabric that entwines families together. Thus, food, cooking and eating become the rituals, traditions and cherished memories that families pass down their lineage. Sharing food makes us, shapes us and ensures that life doesn't break us.

To celebrate this, we have decided to create the first Over60 cookbook. From recipes born out of living off rations during the war, to Country Women's Association baking competitions, cooking is an institution like no other. In this book you can expect a combination of old and new recipes, tradition alongside family secrets and meals for all occasions. We hope this cookbook offers you a journey through time with a collection of tried and cherished recipes. With a combination of recipes from the Over60 community — as well as some we've added — these pages will provide even the most novice of cooks the kitchen prowess that seasoned hostesses possess.

Back to basics

'That's the beautiful thing about food,
it breaks down the barriers.'
— Matt Preston

From cooking terms explained to measurement
conversions, meet your handy kitchen companion
to guide you in the basics of cooking and ensure your
time in the kitchen is a breeze.

Common cooking terms and techniques explained

Al dente (al DEN-tay): Pasta that is cooked but still firm, with fine whitish core showing in the middle. This can take between 8–15 minutes at a rapid boil in an uncovered pan.

Au gratin (oh GRAH-tin): A French term meaning a dish with a browned topping of breadcrumbs and/or grated cheese.

Bake: To cook in an oven.

Bain-marie (bane-mah-REE): A vessel used for keeping food hot prior to service, consisting of a serving pan suspended over hot water.

Bake blind (or blind bake): A technique used for baking an unfilled pastry or tart shell. The pastry shell is lined with baking paper, weighted down with dry beans, rice or pie weights and baked until it's cooked before the filling is added.

Batter: A liquefied mixture of flour and milk or water used to make pancakes and pikelets or to coat foods before frying.

Beurre (burr): French for butter.

Blanch: To drop into boiling water briefly, then drain and cover with iced water to stop the cooking process.

Blend: To combine ingredients with a spoon or spatula using a wide circular motion, mixing to a smooth paste.

Boiling point: When bubbles reach the surface of a liquid and break — 100 degrees Celsius for water.

Bon appetit (Boh nap-pay-TEET): French for 'good appetite', meaning 'I wish you a good meal', or 'enjoy your meal'.

Bouquet garni: A bunch of herbs consisting of parsley, peppercorns, thyme and a bay leaf placed inside a piece of celery and held together with a kitchen twine. This is usually added to stocks, sauces or stews. If dried herbs are used they may be secured in a piece of cheesecloth for easy removal at the end of cooking.

Breadcrumbs — fresh (also known as soft): Crumbs obtained by mincing fresh bread in a food processor; they are softer and give more texture to breaded foods than dry breadcrumbs.

Breadcrumbs — dry: Can be prepared by drying fresh breadcrumbs in an oven or you can get store-bought ones in a packet.

Brown stock: A richly coloured stock made of bones and vegetables, all of which are caramelised before they are simmered in water with seasonings.

Brush-down: To use a pastry brush dipped in cold water to wash down the sides of a pan when making sugar syrup-based products such as toffee.

Brunoise (Broon-WAH): A small cube of approximately 3 mm.

Butterfly cut: To split food, such as boneless meat, fish or shrimp, in half lengthways, leaving the halves joined on one side so that the item spreads open like a book. This is used to increase surface area and speed cooking.

Chiffonade (Shif-fon-NAHD): To finely shred to approximately 3 mm.

Clarified butter (ghee): Purified butterfat; butter is melted and the water and milk solids are removed.

Core: To remove the seeds and casings from fruit and vegetables. Usually performed with a metal apple corer or melon baller.

Coulis (koo-lee): Sauce made from a sieved purée of vegetables or fruit; it may be served hot or cold.

Concassé (con-cass-AY): Peeled, seeded and diced tomatoes.

Creaming: To beat butter and sugar together until light in colour and fluffy in texture.

Croutons: Small squares of bread pan-fried in a little butter and oil and usually served with soup.

Crown roast: A cut of the lamb primal rack; it is formed by tying the ribs in a circle; the tips can be decorated with paper frills and the hollow centre section filled with a stuffing.

Crudités (krew-dee-TAY): Raw vegetables usually served as hors d'oeuvres accompanied by a dipping sauce.

Deglaze: To swirl or stir liquid in a pan to dissolve particles of cooked food remaining on the base of the pan; the resulting mixture often becomes the base for a stock or sauce.

Deep fry: To cook in enough oil to completely immerse the food. Unwatched oil can cause kitchen fires, so be sure not to leave this unattended.

Demi-glace (dem-me-glass): French for half-glaze and used to describe a reduction of equal parts of brown stock and brown sauce by half.

Dice: To cut into small cubes.

Du jour (doo-ZHOOR): French for 'of the day' and used to introduce a menu item that is a special for a particular day, such as a soup.

Egg wash: A mixture of beaten eggs (whole eggs, yolks or whites) and a liquid, usually milk or water, used as part of the crumbing process, or to coat dough/pastry before baking to add a sheen.

En papillote (ahn pap-i-yot): A food (e.g. fish with a vegetable garnish) enclosed in parchment paper or a greased paper wrapper and baked; the paper envelope is usually split open at the table so the diner can enjoy the escaping aroma.

Entrée (ahn-TRAY): A dish served before the main course.

Espresso (ess-PRESS-oh): An Italian coffee-brewing method in which hot water is forced through finely ground and packed coffee under high pressure; the resulting beverage is thick, strong, rich and smooth, but should not be bitter or acidic.

Fillet: An undercut of meat, or a cut of meat or fish without skin or bone.

Fluting: To pinch a pastry edge using forefinger and thumb to create a decorative edge.

Fondant: A type of French confection; also an icing for cakes.

Folding: The process of repeatedly moving a spatula or spoon through a mixture with a cutting motion, lifting and turning the ingredients over to achieve a uniform mixture; often used in the context of adding beaten egg whites.

Food danger zone: The temperature range of 10-60 degrees Celsius, which is most favourable for bacterial growth; also known as the temperature danger zone.

Fricassee (frik-ka-say): A white stew made using milk with white stock.

Frenched: Rack of cutlets or chops, especially lamb, from which the excess fat, meat and connective tissue have been removed from the rib bone, leaving the eye muscle intact.

Galantine (GAL-uhn-teen): A forcemeat of poultry, game, fish, shellfish or suckling pig, wrapped in the skin of the bird or animal, if available, and poached in an appropriate stock; usually served cold in aspic.

Ganache (GAN-nash): A decadently rich and creamy dark chocolate icing of pouring consistency.

Garnish: To decorate food.

Gâteau (gat-TOW): A rich buttery cake, highly decorated and served as a dessert.

Glaze: To brush over liquid with such as an egg wash or a sugar syrup.

Gremolada (greh-mo-LAH-dah): An aromatic garnish of chopped parsley, garlic and lemon zest generally used for osso buco.

Hard-ball stage: A test for the density of sugar syrup; the point at which a small amount of hot syrup forms a rigid ball when dropped into iced water; this is equivalent to 120–130 degrees Celsius or 250–265 degrees Fahrenheit on a sugar thermometer.

Hull: To remove the green end of stem still attached to fruits and vegetables such as strawberries or tomatoes.

Infuse: To steep a seasoning or food in a hot liquid until the liquid absorbs the item's flavour, e.g. a bouquet garni.

Jardinière (zhar-din-AIR): Batons or sticks of fruit or vegetable approximately 5 mm x 5 mm x 20 mm.

Jell test: A method used to test when a jam or jelly is sufficiently cooked, generally by rapidly cooling the boiling mixture to see if it sets.

Julienne: A fine strip of fruit or vegetable approximately 3 mm x 3 mm x 40 mm.

Jus (zhoo): A French term for juice, usually refers to a light sauce.

Jus Lie (zhoo lee-ay): A sauce made by thickening brown stock with cornflour, or a similar starch, and often used like a demi-glaze; also known as fond lie.

Knead — bread dough: To blend a dough by placing it on a floured board and then pressing down using the heel of your hand, pushing the dough away from you then bringing it back in to a ball with the fingertips. The dough should then be turned and the process repeated until the dough becomes satiny and elastic — generally after 5–10 minutes of consistent, energetic kneading.

Knead — pastry: To blend a firm dough, place it on a floured surface and lightly press down with the heel of the palm, then rotate and repeat a few times just until the dough comes together.

Legumes: A large group of plants that have double-seamed pods containing a single row of seeds; depending on the variety, the seeds, the pod and seeds together or the dried seeds are eaten.

Macédoine (mas-eh-doine): A dice or cube approximately 8 mm x 8 mm.

Mask: To cover or coat with a thick sauce.

Marinade: A highly seasoned liquid made of oils, herbs and vinegar in which meat or poultry is soaked for some time to impart flavour and tenderise.

Marinate: To cover food in a marinade and allow to stand for a period of time before cooking to allow flavours to develop.

Mesclun (MEHS-kluhn): A mixture of several kinds of salad greens, especially baby lettuces; although there is no set standard, the mixture usually includes baby red cos, endive, mache, oak leaf, radicchio and rocket, among others.

Mise en place (meese-en-plaz): French for 'putting in place' and used to describe the preparation and assembly of all necessary ingredients and equipment before cooking.

Mirepoix (Mirror-pwah): A rough cut or chop of vegetables used as a stock base; usually consisting of onions, carrots and celery.

Muslin bag: Small cloth bag used to hold fresh or dried herbs, as for a bouquet garni, which is submerged into liquid ingredients to infuse flavours.

Oxidation: A chemical reaction caused by exposure to oxygen, usually discolouring the cut surfaces of foods such as potatoes and apples.

Panada: A very thick white sauce used to bind meat or fish for rissoles or croquettes.

Pastry rose: Pastry garnish formed from fresh pastry and attached to a savoury pie for decoration.

Pâte sucrée (pat-soo-kray): A dough containing sugar that produces a very rich, crisp (not flaky) baked product, it is used for tart shells; also known as sweet dough.

Paysanne: Thinly sliced shapes of fruit or vegetable, either triangular, square or round, approximately 15 mm x 3 mm.

Pith: The bitter white cellulose material found on and around citrus fruits just under the skin.

Poaching: To cook in water that is heated to approximately 70–80 degrees Celsius.

Prove: To allow a yeast dough to rest in a warm place and double in size.

Purée: A pulp made by forcing cooked fruits or vegetables through a strainer or placing into a food processor or blender.

Reduce: To cook a liquid mixture, often a sauce, until the quantity decreases through evaporation; typically done to concentrate flavours and thicken liquids.

Reduction: A sauce or other liquid that has been reduced.

Roast: To cook in an oven, normally applies to joints of meat or poultry.

Roux (roo): A cooked mixture of equal parts, by weight, of plain flour and fat used as a thickener for sauces, soups and other dishes; cooking the flour in fat coats the starch granules with the fat and prevents them from forming lumps when liquid is introduced.

Rub-in: To break up solid fat into flour and then rub between the fingertips until the fat and flour mixture resembles breadcrumbs.

Sabayon (sab-be-yon): A foamy, stirred French custard sauce made by whisking eggs, sugar and wine over low heat; known in Italian as zabaglione.

Sauté: To fry in a small amount of hot oil and butter until soft and lightly browned.

Score: To make shallow cuts in meat or fish, usually in a diamond pattern; done for decorative purposes, to assist in absorbing flavours and to tenderise the product.

Sear: To brown food quickly over high heat; usually done as a preparatory step for combination cooking methods.

Shallow fry: To cook on the stovetop in a pan in approximately 0.5 mm of oil.

Simmer: To cook over a low heat so that liquid in a pan forms unbroken bubbles or bubbles gently.

Soft-ball stage: A test for the density of sugar syrup; the point at which a small amount of hot syrup will form a soft sticky ball when dropped in cold water.

Soft-crack stage: A test for the density of sugar syrup; the point at which a small amount of hot syrup will separate into firm but bendable strands when dropped in cold water.

Steaming: To cook over a pan of boiling water without immersing food in the water; the food to be steamed can be cooked in any of four commonly used vessels — double saucepan with perforated steamer insert, metal colander over saucepan, bamboo basket over saucepan or bench-top electrical steaming appliance.

Sterilising jars: Method used to assure that bottles and lids are free from dirt and bacteria. Can be achieved using the dry heat method in the oven or moist heat when jars and lids are boiled.

Stir-fry: A very quick method of cookery in which food is tossed, or constantly and briskly stirred, in a small amount of oil in a wok or pan over a very high heat (a gas flame gives the best results).

Tamping (of a tin): After placing a cake batter into a tin/pan, the tin is firmly tapped onto a bench top or firm surface to remove excess air bubbles before baking.

Trussing (poultry): Using sterile kitchen twine to secure the wings and drumsticks of a bird to the rest of the carcass.

Vanilla sugar: Blending of caster sugar with dry vanilla bean pod. Store in a screw-top jar.

Velouté sauce (ver-loo-TAY): French sauce made by thickening a veal, chicken or fish stock with a golden roux; also known as a blond sauce.

Water bath: A heatproof vessel which is half-filled with water and used to cook baked custards or soufflé.

Well: A hole or depression in dry ingredients to which wet ingredients are added.

Whisk: To aerate a mixture using a metal or plastic balloon whisk.

Zest: The coloured, outermost layer of citrus rind; also the action of removing strips of rind from a citrus fruit. Used for flavouring creams, custards and baked goods; it can be candied and used as a confection or decoration.

Conversions

Temperatures

100 degrees Celsius (boiling point) – 212 degrees Fahrenheit
0 degrees Celsius (freezing point) – 32 degrees Fahrenheit

Celsius (C.)	Fahrenheit (F.)	Gas Mark	
120°	250°	1	Very slow
150°	300°	2	Slow
160°	325°	3	Moderately slow
180°	350°	4	Moderate
190°	375°	5	Moderately hot
200°	400°	6	Hot
230°	450°	7	Very hot
250°	500°	9	Very hot

Liquid conversions

1 gill	150 ml	⅔ cup
½ pint	300 ml	1¼ cups
1 pint	600 ml	2½ cups
1 quart	1L + 150 ml	4½ cups
1 gallon	4L+ 500 ml	18 cups

Metric and spoon measurements

1 metric cup	250 ml
1 tablespoon	20 ml
1 teaspoon	5 ml
½ teaspoon	2.5 ml
¼ teaspoon	1.25 ml

Breakfast to brunch

*'There are rules around everything in life and to put strict,
extreme rules on food too makes me sad.'*
— Donna Hay

Nutritionally speaking, it is commonly thought that
breakfast is the most important meal of the day.
However, we'd like to argue that there's an ever more
important reason — to feed the soul so you can take on
the day and whatever life has to throw at you. And with
that, here are a collection of delicious — and sometimes
naughty — recipes to help you make an 'occasion' out of
breakfast and brunch.

Banana pikelets

*Enjoy a sweet start to the day by indulging in
these scrumptious banana pikelets.*

MAKES: 8

1 egg
1 banana, plus extra to serve
½ cup soft brown sugar
¾ cup milk
½ teaspoon vanilla extract

1¼ cups wholemeal self-raising
 flour
1 teaspoon margarine spread
honey or maple syrup, to serve

1. Whisk the egg in a small bowl using a fork.

2. In a separate bowl, mash the banana and then add the egg,
    sugar, milk and vanilla. Stir in the flour and allow to sit for
    a few minutes until the flour absorbs some of the milk and
    the mixture thickens slightly.

3. Heat a frying pan over medium–high heat. Add the
    margarine spread and pour 3 tablespoons of the pikelet
    mixture into the pan. After about 1½ minutes, when bubbles
    appear on the uncooked surface, turn the pikelets over and
    cook the other side for a further 2 minutes. Place the cooked
    pikelets on paper towels until all pikelets are cooked.

4. Serve with the honey or maple syrup and extra banana.

    Note: Sprinkle with nuts – like hazelnuts or Brazil nuts –
    to add a protein kick to your pikelets.

Delicious salmon spread

'This is so easy to make and everyone loves it. It can be used on crackers, biscuits or bread.' Maree Brown

SERVES: 8–10

1 x 210 g tin pink salmon, drained

250 g cream cheese, at room temperature

2 tablespoons tomato sauce

1 tablespoon worcestershire sauce

1 small onion, finely chopped

parsley, chopped (optional)

1. Mix all the ingredients together in a large bowl.

2. Cover with plastic wrap and refrigerate until ready to serve.

   Note 1: You can store this in the refrigerator in an airtight container for up to three days.

   Note 2: To make this healthy, opt for low-fat cream cheese.

Apricot bran loaf

'This recipe went around during my mothers' club days at my kids' primary school. It was always a favourite.' Lyn Batson

SERVES: 10–12

I cup chopped dried apricots
I cup milk
I cup unprocessed bran

I cup sugar
I cup self-raising flour

1. Add the apricots, milk, bran and sugar to a bowl and stir to combine. Cover with plastic wrap and refrigerate overnight.

2. Mix in the self-raising flour. Preheat the oven to 180°C. Lightly grease a 20 cm x 10 cm loaf tin and line with baking paper.

3. Pour the mixture into the tin and bake for 35 minutes, or until a skewer comes out clean when inserted in the centre.

4. Leave to cool in the tin for 5 minutes, then turn out onto a wire rack to cool completely. To serve, slice and spread with butter.

The Way Mum Made It

Banana and walnut overnight oats

These oats are so full of flavour and sweetness that you probably won't even realise just how healthy they are. With a mix of seeds and nuts you can swap for things you have on hand, this is a truly versatile breakfast you'll love.

SERVES: 1

½ cup steel-cut oats or rolled oats

1 teaspoon chia seeds

1 teaspoon flaxseeds

½ teaspoon cinnamon

¼ teaspoon nutmeg

2 tablespoons chopped walnuts

2 teaspoons maple syrup or honey

½ cup milk

½ teaspoon vanilla extract

1 banana, to serve

1. Mix the dry ingredients together in a bowl until well combined.

2. Add the syrup or honey, milk and vanilla and stir. Cover with plastic wrap and refrigerate overnight.

3. Top with sliced banana and serve.

Zucchini slice

'I starting making this many years ago for my family and now my friends love it too. People have tried to make it but they say it's not like mine. When I make it for people there is never any left over.' Jeannie Keeble

SERVES: 20

8 eggs
1 cup grated tasty cheese
¾ cup thick cream
10 bacon rashers, cooked and
 chopped into small pieces
6 spring onions, chopped

2 cups chopped flat-leaf parsley
2 cups self-raising flour
2 tablespoons oil
4 zucchini, grated
2 carrots, grated

1. Preheat the oven to 180°C. Line a lasagne dish with baking paper.

2. In a bowl, combine the eggs, cheese and cream and whisk together.

3. Add the bacon, spring onions, parsley, flour and oil. Mix well to combine. Add the zucchini and carrot.

4. Pour the mixture into the prepared lasagne dish. Bake for 45–60 minutes, or until cooked through. Allow to cool before slicing and serving.

Apple fritters

To add a little sweetness to breakfast or brunch why not try these fun delights? Apple fritters make great snacks or a quick dessert too.

SERVES: 2

2 cups canola oil

⅔ cup plain flour

I teaspoon baking powder

⅛ teaspoon salt

3 tablespoons sugar

½ teaspoon cinnamon

4 tablespoons thick cream

I tablespoon melted unsalted butter

I large egg

I small apple, peeled and finely diced

icing sugar, to serve

1. Heat the oil in a large deep pan over medium heat.

2. In a bowl, whisk together the flour, baking powder, salt, sugar and cinnamon.

3. In another bowl, lightly whisk together the cream, butter and egg.

4. Add the wet mixture to the dry mixture, stirring lightly, and then fold in the diced apple.

5. Ensure the oil is hot. Use a ½-cup measure to scoop out I fritter. Press the batter firmly into the measuring cup, and then place the batter in your hand and press it flat. Repeat with the remaining batter.

6. Fry the fritters for 3 minutes on each side, or until golden brown. Remove from the oil with a slotted spoon and drain on paper towels.

7. Dust with icing sugar before serving.

Five-cup loaf

'This was my late father's favourite recipe. He used to make two or three at a time and freeze them. It's good for you too.' Julie Unsworth

MAKES: 1 LOAF

1 cup self-raising flour
1 cup mixed dried fruit
1 cup soft brown sugar

1 cup All-Bran
1 cup milk

1. Preheat the oven to 180°C. Lightly grease a loaf tin.

2. Mix all the dry ingredients together thoroughly. Add the milk and mix well. Leave the mixture to stand for up to 1 hour.

3. Pour the mixture into the tin and bake for 1 hour, or until the mixture comes away from the sides of the tin. Cool on a wire rack.

4. Cut into slices and serve with or without butter.

   Note: This loaf can be frozen for up to 1 month.

Simple baked eggs in chunky tomato sauce

This Spanish-style vegetarian dish is hearty, healthy and perfect for breakfast or brunch on the weekends.

SERVES: 2

oil, for frying
½ onion, diced
1 capsicum, stemmed, seeded, and finely diced
2 garlic cloves, minced
1 x 400 g tin crushed tomatoes

chilli flakes (optional)
salt and pepper, to season
2 eggs
chopped coriander, to garnish
fresh crusty bread, to serve

1. Preheat the oven to 200°C.

2. Heat the oil in a frying pan over medium heat. Add the onion and capsicum and stir for 8–10 minutes, or until softened.

3. Add the garlic and cook for 2 minutes, or until fragrant.

4. Stir in the tomatoes and simmer for 10 minutes. Add a pinch of chilli flakes (if using). Season with salt and pepper to taste.

5. Divide the sauce between two shallow baking dishes. Make a well in the centre of each dish using a spoon and crack an egg into each well.

6. Place in the oven and bake for 10 minutes, or until the egg whites are cooked through but the yolks are still soft and runny. Top with the coriander and serve with a side of crusty bread.

Cheese scones

*If you thought scones were all about the sweet variety,
think again. Hot out of the oven with a spreading of
butter on top, these cheesy scones are heaven.*

MAKES: 15

3 cups self-raising flour
pinch of salt
60 g butter, chilled, chopped

⅔ cup coarsely grated cheddar
   cheese
1½ cups buttermilk, plus extra
   to glaze

1. Preheat the oven to 220°C. Lightly flour a baking tray.

2. Combine the flour and salt in a large bowl. Use your
    fingertips to rub the butter into the flour until the mixture
    resembles fine breadcrumbs. Stir in the cheese.

3. Add the buttermilk and mix until just combined by using a
    round-bladed knife in a cutting motion. Use your hands to
    bring the dough together in the bowl.

4. Turn the dough out onto a lightly floured surface. Knead
    gently until smooth. Use the palm of your hand to flatten
    until about 2 cm thick. Use a round 5.5 cm diameter pastry
    cutter to cut 15 discs from the dough. Place about 1 cm apart
    on the baking tray. Gently brush the tops with a little extra
    buttermilk to glaze.

5. Bake for 12 minutes, or until the scones are golden and sound hollow when tapped on top. Serve warm with butter.

Note: Scones can be stored in the freezer in an airtight container or zip-lock bag for up to 2 months.

Corn fritters

Simple to make, these corn fritters will delight both young and old. Serve in the morning for an extra-special breakfast.

MAKES: 8

1 cup self-raising flour
2 tablespoons cornflour
2 eggs, separated
3 tablespoons milk
250 g sweetcorn

2 spring onions, finely chopped
salt and pepper, to season
1 tablespoon oil
sour cream, to serve (optional)

1. Sift the flour and cornflour into a bowl. Add the egg yolks and milk and mix well.

2. Whip the egg whites until stiff and gently fold into the flour mixture. Stir in the corn and spring onion and season with salt and pepper.

3. Heat the oil in a frying pan over high heat. Drop a generous tablespoon of the mixture into the pan and spread to approximately 8 cm in diameter. Cook until golden brown, turn and cook the other side. Drain on paper towels. Repeat with the remaining mixture.

4. Serve warm with sour cream, if desired.

Homemade raisin bread

Who doesn't love a nice hot slice of raisin toast with butter?

SERVES: 6–8

2 teaspoons dried yeast
¼ cup soft brown sugar
I cup warm water
I cup wholemeal flour
I½ cups plain flour
2 teaspoons bread improver

2 teaspoons mixed spice
I teaspoon salt
I cup raisins
¼ cup mixed peel
I egg yolk
I tablespoon milk

1. In a bowl, combine the yeast and I tablespoon of brown sugar with the water. Set this aside.

2. Combine the flours with the bread improver, mixed spice, remaining sugar, and salt in a large bowl. Make a well in the centre and pour the yeast mixture into it. Using a wooden spoon, stir to combine.

3. Turn the dough out onto a lightly floured surface and knead for I0–I5 minutes — the dough should become smooth and elastic/stretchy.

4. Place the dough in a large bowl, and cover loosely with a tea towel or plastic wrap. Leave in a warm place for I hour, or until the dough has doubled in size.

5. Punch down the dough and turn it out onto a lightly floured surface. Add the raisins and mixed peel and knead until the fruit is evenly distributed throughout the dough.

6. Preheat the oven to 220°C and lightly grease a 10 cm x 20 cm loaf tin.

7. Shape your dough into a log and place in the tin. Set aside for a further 30 minutes to double in size.

8. Make an egg wash with the egg yolk and milk, and brush over the top of the dough.

9. Bake the bread for 10 minutes, then reduce the heat to 180°C and bake for a further 20 minutes. If you're not confident the loaf is done, tap the base — it should sound hollow.

10. Allow the loaf to cool on a wire rack. Cut into slices and serve toasted.

Extra sour lemon ice tea

*'I came up with this last year when I realised that in my lemon
tree pot there is also a lemon balm herb growing. And because I
love eating and drinking sour things, especially when it's hot, I had
the idea to make a drink from my produce.' Petra Engelhardt*

MAKES: 1 LITRE

2 lemons
20 lemon tree leaves
10 lemon balm leaves

3 cups boiling water
1 cup cold sparkling water

1. Squeeze the juice of 1 lemon into an ice cube tray and place
    in the freezer. As a decorative addition you can also add a
    small lemon tree leaf in each ice cube mould.

2. Place the lemon tree leaves and lemon balm leaves in a heat-
    resistant jug and pour the boiling water over them. Let it
    cool down and then place it in the fridge for at least 5 hours.

3. Before serving, take out the leaves and pour the juice of the
    second lemon and the sparkling water into the jug and drop
    the lemon ice cubes in.

    Note 1: Leaves of lemon balm can be purchased online
    or at some specialty health food shops.

    Note 2: If this ice tea is too sour for you, add 2 teaspoons
    of cane sugar into your glass.

Healthy banana and walnut muffins

*Fact: Everyone likes muffins. Fact: They're not the healthiest
snack. Until now. You won't be able to get enough of
these treats packed with wholesome goodness.*

MAKES: 24

4 ripe bananas, chopped
I cup soft brown sugar
½ cup walnut oil
I large egg
I cup plain flour
I cup wholemeal flour

I teaspoon baking powder
I teaspoon bicarbonate of soda
½ teaspoon coarse salt
½ cup non-fat yoghurt
I tablespoon vanilla extract
I cup chopped toasted walnuts

1. Preheat the oven to 180°C. Line 24 x ⅓-cup capacity muffin
   tin holes with paper cases.

3. Using an electric mixer, beat the banana on medium speed
   until mashed. Add in the sugar, oil and egg and continue to
   beat until smooth.

4. Reduce the speed to low and add the flours, baking powder,
   bicarbonate of soda and salt. Beat until smooth.

5. Add in the yoghurt and vanilla and beat until combined.
   Fold in the walnuts.

6. Spoon the mixture into the paper cases until three-quarters full. Bake for 20 minutes, or until a skewer inserted into the centre comes out clean.

Potato and fennel tarte tatin

*This tasty tart looks fantastic, and is so simple to make. Just
a few ingredients and you've got one hell of a side dish.*

SERVES: 4

4 small potatoes (either new or
  pontiac)
2 large fennel bulbs
2 tablespoons olive oil

salt and pepper, to season
4 tablespoons chicken stock
1 sheet frozen puff pastry

1. Preheat the oven to 220°C. Thinly slice the potatoes (use a
    mandolin for consistency), and chop the fennel into wedges.

2. Heat half the oil in a 22 cm ovenproof frying pan over
    medium heat.

3. Cook the potatoes, in batches, for 1 minute on each side, or
    until they are lightly golden brown. Set aside until needed.

4. Heat the remaining oil in the pan and add the fennel. Cook
    for 2–3 minutes, turning, until golden brown and tender.

5. Remove the pan from the heat. Arrange the potato and
    fennel in layers in the pan. Season with salt and pepper
    between the layers.

6. Drizzle the stock over the top, taking care to distribute
    evenly.

7. Place the pastry over the potato and fennel, and tuck in the
    excess. Bake for 15 minutes, or until the pastry is golden.

8. Carefully turn the tart out, pastry-side down, onto a serving plate or cutting board. Cut into wedges and serve immediately.

Baked sticky date apples

*When it comes to the perfect addition to brunch, sometimes
you should look no further than fruit. With a few simple
ingredients you can make something truly special.*

SERVES: 4

4 apples (such as golden
   delicious or granny smith)
1 tablespoon lemon juice
⅓ cup pitted dates, chopped
2 teaspoons vanilla extract

2 tablespoons soft brown sugar
2 tablespoons almonds,
   toasted, roughly chopped
1 teaspoon mixed spice
custard, to serve

1. Preheat the oven to 180°C.

2. Using a small, sharp knife, remove the cores from the
   apples. You can either leave the apples whole with the bases
   intact or you can cut the top off — almost so you have a lid.

3. Place the apples, upright, in a ceramic baking dish and
   drizzle the lemon juice into the apple holes.

4. Combine the dates, vanilla, sugar, almonds and spice.
   Spoon the mixture into centre of each apple. Cover with
   foil.

5. Bake for 15 minutes, then remove the foil. Bake for a further
   10–15 minutes, or until the apples are tender. Serve warm
   with the custard.

Homemade baked beans

'Beans are an excellent source of protein and fibre and cooking them yourself means they are healthier and better for your digestive systems. This recipe makes an old favourite taste even better; a great option for an after-school snack for the grandkids.' Anne Taylor

SERVES: 2–4

1½ cups haricot beans
1 tablespoon olive oil
2 onions, chopped
2 garlic cloves, finely chopped
1 x 400 g tin whole tomatoes, chopped or mixed in a blender

2 tablespoons tomato paste
2 tablespoons honey
2 tablespoons soy sauce
2 teaspoons basil
1 teaspoon marjoram
¼ teaspoon thyme
1 cup water

1. Fill a large saucepan with 1.5 litres of water and add the beans. Bring to the boil over medium heat and boil for 2 minutes. Leave to stand for 1–2 hours, then discard the water.

2. Add another 1.5 litres of water and simmer for 1 hour 20 minutes before discarding the water. (Alternatively, you can use tinned beans available from most supermarkets.)

3. Add the oil, onion and garlic to a saucepan over medium heat and cook, stirring, until browned.

4. Add the remaining ingredients and stir until boiling. Reduce the heat and simmer for 15 minutes. If the mixture appears to thicken at any stage, add some additional water.

Note: Serve as an accompaniment to another dish or as a nutritious snack.

Fluffy blueberry pancakes

*For a special weekend breakfast, these pancakes are worth
the one-hour wait while the batter works its magic.*

MAKES: 12

1¼ cups plain flour
pinch of salt
1 tablespoon baking powder
1 teaspoon sugar
1 egg
1 cup milk

1 tablespoon butter, melted
½ cup blueberries (thawed if
    frozen)
olive oil spray
honey or maple syrup, to serve

1. Sift the flour, salt, baking powder and sugar into a bowl. Add the egg, milk and butter and stir to combine.

2. Gently fold in the blueberries and set the batter aside for 1 hour.

3. Heat a large non-stick frying pan over medium–high heat. Spray the pan with olive oil spray.

4. Using 3 tablespoons mixture per pancake, cook 2 pancakes for 3–4 minutes, or until bubbles appear on the surface. Turn and cook for 3 minutes, or until cooked through. Transfer to a plate. Cover loosely with foil to keep warm. Repeat with the remaining mixture.

5. Serve with the honey or maple syrup.

Garlic and herb pull-apart bread

Perfect as an accompaniment on the breakfast or brunch table, this garlic and herb pull-apart bread is sure to become a fast favourite in your house.

MAKES: I LOAF

3½ cups bread flour
I tablespoon sugar
2¼ teaspoons rapid rise yeast
1¼ teaspoons sea salt
pinch of dried thyme
8 garlic cloves
1½ teaspoons dried basil

3 tablespoons milk
I cup + 2 tablespoons warm water
2 tablespoons olive oil
4 tablespoons unsalted butter, melted
½ cup grated parmesan cheese

1. Combine the flour, sugar, yeast, salt, thyme, two minced garlic cloves and ½ teaspoon basil in a large mixing bowl.

2. Using an electric mixer on low, add the milk, water and olive oil. Increase the speed as needed until the dough pulls away from the sides of the bowl. Shape into a ball.

3. Place the dough in a large greased bowl. Cover and place in a warm area until it has doubled in size.

4. Roll the dough out to form a 30 cm x 50 cm rectangle. Brush generously with 3 tablespoons of the melted butter. Sprinkle with the remaining basil, parmesan cheese and minced garlic.

5. Cut the dough into six strips and layer on top of each other. Cut this into six equal stacks. Transfer these stacks to a lightly greased 10.5 cm x 25 cm loaf tin. Cover loosely and allow to rise for about 1 hour.

6. Preheat the oven to 175°C. Drizzle the loaf with the remaining melted butter. Bake for 35 minutes. Cover with foil if necessary to prevent burning. Serve warm.

Kiwifruit and rockmelon smoothie

SERVES: 1

1 granny smith apple, peeled
  and chopped
1 kiwifruit, peeled and chopped
1¾ cups rockmelon pieces

1 tablespoon honey
1 tablespoon lemon juice
1 cup ice cubes

1. Place the fruit, honey and lemon juice in a blender and blend until smooth.

2. Add the ice cubes and blend until the smoothie is a slushy, icy consistency. Serve immediately.

Ham and cheese galettes

*With the strong flavour of ham and the gooeyness of melted cheese,
these galettes will go down a treat with children and adults alike.*

SERVES: 4

1 cup plain flour
½ teaspoon sea salt
1 egg
2 cups water

50 g butter
250 g grated Emmental cheese
4 slices leg ham, roughly torn

1. Combine the flour, salt and egg in a large bowl. Stir to combine, then slowly whisk in the water. The batter should be the consistency of light cream. If it's too thick, slowly add more water.

2. Heat a large non-stick frying pan over medium–high heat. Add 10 g of the butter, then pour ½ cup of batter into the pan and quickly swirl around so it coats the pan thinly and evenly.

3. Cook the galette for about 2 minutes or until the borders peel off and the bottom is slightly brown. Flip over and cook the other side for 1 minute. Repeat with the remaining batter. Pile the galettes onto a warm plate.

4. Return a galette to the pan, sprinkle a quarter of the cheese over the surface of the galette and when it has melted, add a quarter of the ham. Roll over the borders and serve. Repeat with the remaining galettes.

Raspberry banana bread with passionfruit icing

When you're planning an extra-special breakfast or having people over for brunch, you're going to want to indulge. This delightful raspberry and banana bread with passionfruit icing is the perfect way to do that.

SERVES: 10

1–2 tablespoons melted butter,
  to grease
125 g unsalted butter, chopped
⅔ cup soft brown sugar
2 eggs, lightly whisked
½ cup sour cream
1 cup mashed ripe banana
1½ cups self-raising flour
1 teaspoon cinnamon
¼ teaspoon bicarbonate of soda

100 g frozen raspberries
fresh raspberries, to serve
Icing
125 g cream cheese, at room
  temperature
40 g unsalted butter, at room
  temperature
½ cup icing sugar
3 tablespoons fresh passionfruit
  pulp

1. Preheat the oven to 180°C. Brush a 10 cm x 20 cm loaf tin with the melted butter. Line the base with non-stick baking paper.

2. Stir the butter and sugar in a small saucepan over low heat until the butter melts. Set aside for 10 minutes to cool slightly.

3. Stir the egg, sour cream and banana into the butter mixture. Sift the flour, cinnamon and bicarbonate of soda into a large bowl. Make a well in the centre. Add the banana mixture and stir until well combined. Fold in the frozen raspberries.

4. Spoon the mixture into the prepared tin. Bake for 1 hour 10 minutes, or until a skewer inserted into the centre comes out clean. Leave to cool in the tin for 5 minutes before transferring to a wire rack to cool completely.

5. To make the icing, use an electric mixer to beat the cream cheese, butter and icing sugar until pale and creamy. Beat in half the passionfruit pulp.

6. Spread the icing over the cake. Top with the raspberries and drizzle over the remaining passionfruit pulp.

Broccoli quiche

Hearty and healthy, this broccoli quiche is packed full of
wholesome goodness and has plenty of flavour to boot.

SERVES: 6

Pastry
1¼ cups plain flour
¼ cup polenta
125 g chilled butter, chopped
1 egg
2 teaspoons cold water
Filling
20 g butter

2 leeks, white part only, washed
    and thinly sliced
300 ml thick cream
3 eggs
2 egg yolks
salt and pepper, to season
½ cup grated cheddar cheese
250 g broccoli, cut into florets

1. To make the pastry, process the flour, polenta and butter in
    a food processor until the mixture resembles breadcrumbs.
    Add the egg and water and process until a dough forms.
    Shape into a circle and wrap in plastic wrap. Place in the
    refrigerator for 20 minutes.

2. To start on the filling, melt the butter in a frying pan over
    medium heat. Add the leek and cook for 5–8 minutes,
    stirring, until softened but not brown. Set aside to cool.

3. Preheat the oven to 200°C. Grease a 22 cm loose-based tart
    tin. Roll out the pastry on a lightly floured surface until
    3 mm thick. Ease into the prepared tin. Trim the edge and
    prick the base with a fork. Refrigerate for 10 minutes.

4. Line the pastry with baking paper and fill with rice (or pastry weights). Blind bake for 15 minutes. Remove the paper and rice (or weights) and bake for a further 5 minutes, or until the pastry is dry.

5. Whisk together the cream, eggs and egg yolks. Season.

6. Spread the leek over the pastry shell. Scatter over half of the cheddar and then the broccoli. Carefully pour over the egg mixture and top with the remaining cheddar.

7. Bake for 10 minutes. Reduce the oven to 180°C and bake for a further 30 minutes, or until set. Serve warm.

Tomato, feta, ham and rosemary muffins

Great for an on-the-run breakfast, these savoury muffins work equally as well for brunch in the park — they will disappear in no time at all.

MAKES: 12

¾ cup self-raising flour
salt and pepper
1 egg, lightly beaten
90 g shaved ham, chopped
6 cherry tomatoes, halved

⅔ cup grated feta cheese
4 tablespoons milk
2 tablespoons olive oil
2 tablespoons rosemary leaves,
    plus 12 small sprigs

1. Preheat the oven to 200°C. Lightly grease a 12-hole mini muffin tin.

2. Place the flour and salt and pepper in a large bowl.

3. Place the egg, ham, tomatoes, feta, milk, olive oil and rosemary leaves in a separate bowl. Mix until combined. Add the ham and cheese mixture to the flour and fold lightly until just combined.

4. Spoon the mixture into the muffin holes. Press a sprig of rosemary in the top of each muffin. Bake for 15–18 minutes, or until golden.

Maple baked pears

*These delicious baked pears make a show-stopping addition
for AM meals — and are surprisingly simple to prepare.*

SERVES: 4

4 pears, cut in half lengthways
2 tablespoons water
2 tablespoons maple syrup

1 teaspoon cinnamon
4 whole star anise
¼ cup crushed walnuts

1. Preheat the oven to 200°C. Place the pears in a baking dish.

2. In a small jug, combine the water and maple syrup. Stir in
   the cinnamon and star anise. Pour this mixture over the
   pears and scatter the walnuts over the top.

3. Bake for 30 minutes, turning once. The pears should
   be tender when done. Serve with yoghurt and muesli, if
   desired.

   Note: To make this for one person, divide ingredients by
   four.

Asparagus ribbon tart

*Combining delicate ribbons of fresh asparagus with
a delicious cheesy tart filling, this puff pastry delight
will win your heart as well as your taste buds.*

SERVES: 6

3 eggs
105 ml milk
1 sheet puff pastry

75 g grated cheddar cheese
200 g asparagus, trimmed and
sliced into ribbons

1. Preheat the oven to 160°C. Grease a 6 cm deep loose-based tart tin.

2. Whisk the eggs together in a bowl. Add the milk and whisk again.

3. Line the tin with the puff pastry and sprinkle a little grated cheese over the base.

4. Lay the asparagus in the tin and pour the egg mixture over the top along with the remaining cheese (do this slowly – depending on the size of your tin, you may not need all of the mixture).

5. Bake for 15–20 minutes, or until the pastry is puffed and golden and the egg is set.

Mini fruit tarts

*These tarts are tasty crowd–pleasers that are sure to
impress. You can make your own pastry, or opt for
store–bought shortcrust to make things easier.*

SERVES: 8

seasonal fruits of your choice,
  to serve

Pastry

100 g unsalted butter, cubed

200 g plain flour

3–4 tablespoons cold water

Filling (crème pâtissière)

300 ml low-fat milk

3 egg yolks

1½ teaspoons vanilla extract

100 g caster sugar

2 tablespoons plain flour

1. To make the pastry, use a food processer to blend the butter
    and flour until they resemble breadcrumbs. Slowly add the
    water and mix again. Refrigerate for at least 30 minutes.
    Roll the pastry out between two sheets of plastic wrap until it
    is 2.5 mm thick. Preheat the oven to 180°C.

2. Cut the pastry to size and line 8 mini tart tins. Trim the
    edges and prick the base of the pastry with a fork. Line the
    pastry with baking paper and fill with pastry weights or rice.
    Blind bake for 12 minutes. Remove the baking paper and
    weights or rice and bake for a further 12 minutes, or until
    the pastry is lightly golden. Set aside to cool completely.

3. To make the filling, heat the milk in a saucepan over medium heat until warm (do not boil). In a large bowl, whisk together the egg yolks, vanilla and sugar. When the mixture is smooth, sift in the flour and stir to combine. Slowly add the warm milk to the mixture, continuously whisking. Pour the mixture back into the saucepan and gently bring to the boil while continuing to whisk. When the mixture is thick and creamy, remove from the heat and set aside to cool.

4. Fill the cooled tart bases with the filling and arrange your chosen fruits on top to serve.

Caramelised onion and sweet potato tart

*Complete with caramelised onion, sweet potato and feta cheese,
this crunchy puff pastry tart will make your mouth water.*

SERVES: 8

I large sheet frozen puff pastry,
thawed

I tablespoon olive oil

3 onions, halved and sliced

500 g sweet potato

100 g reduced-fat feta cheese,
crumbled

4 eggs, lightly beaten

I tablespoon thyme leaves

1. Preheat the oven to 180°C. Line a 22 cm loose-based flan
    tin (round or square) with the pastry and trim the edges.

2. Line the pastry with a sheet of baking paper and fill with
    dried beans or rice. Bake for 15 minutes, then remove the
    paper and beans or rice and bake for a further 10 minutes.
    Cool slightly.

3. Meanwhile, heat the oil in a large frying pan over medium
    heat and add the onion. Cook for 15 minutes, stirring
    occasionally, until deep golden brown.

4. Peel the sweet potato and cut into 2 cm cubes. Steam or
    microwave until tender.

5. Fill the tart shell with the onion, sweet potato and feta cheese.

6. Pour the egg over and sprinkle with the thyme. Bake for 40–45 minutes, or until the egg has set. Serve warm or at room temperature.

Blueberry muffins

Bursting with berry goodness, these are delicious
served warm with a cup of tea or coffee.

MAKES: 18

115 g unsalted butter, at room
  temperature
1 cup sugar
2 large eggs
1 teaspoon vanilla extract
2 teaspoons baking powder

¼ teaspoon salt
2 cups plain flour
½ cup milk
2½-3 cups blueberries (fresh
  or frozen)

1. Preheat the oven to 190°C. Lightly grease an 18-hole muffin
    tin.

2. Using an electric mixer, beat the butter in a large bowl until
    creamy. Add the sugar and continue to beat until light and
    fluffy.

3. Add the eggs one at a time, beating after each addition. Beat
    in the vanilla extract, baking powder and salt.

4. Using a metal spoon, gently fold in half of the flour. When it
    is incorporated, fold in half of the milk. Repeat this process
    with the remaining flour and milk.

5. Add the blueberries and gently fold until they are evenly distributed throughout the batter. Spoon the mixture into the muffin holes.

6. Bake for 15–20 minutes, or until golden brown and springy to the touch. Allow to cool for a few minutes before serving warm.

Filomena's health bread

Filomena Wollensack

MAKES: 2–3 LOAVES

1 litre warm water
3 teaspoons yeast
3 tablespoons olive oil
1 teaspoon sugar
2 tablespoons salt
1 cup ground almonds

½ cup sesame seeds
½ cup linseeds (flaxseeds)
½ cup pumpkin seeds
3 tablespoons sunflower seeds
1 cup rolled oats
1 kg plain flour, plus extra

1. Combine the warm water, yeast, oil, sugar and salt in a large bowl. Add the almonds, seeds and oats and mix well.

2. Fold in the flour. Turn the dough out onto a lightly floured surface and knead for about 2 minutes.

3. Place the dough back in the bowl. Cover with plastic wrap, then cover with a wool blanket. Leave the dough to rise for 2 hours, or until doubled in size.

4. Turn the dough out onto a lightly floured surface and roll.

5. Cut the dough into 180 g portions, then roll each portion into a wide sausage. Flatten each portion so it's as wide and thick as your hand.

6. Heat a large frying pan over low heat. Add two portions of the dough, cover with a lid, and cook for 6 minutes on each side. Remove from the pan and set aside to cool. Repeat with the remaining portions.

The Way Mum Made It

7. Store in the fridge for up to 5 days until needed. Before serving, toast the bread in the toaster.

    Note: This bread can also be frozen. Store in an airtight container.

Smoked salmon bagels with cream cheese

SERVES: 4–6

250 g cream cheese

1 tablespoon water

1 teaspoon freshly squeezed
lemon juice

1 teaspoon lemon zest

2 teaspoons chopped dill

4–6 bagels of your choice

200 g smoked salmon

2 handfuls rocket

1. Using an electric mixer, mix the cream cheese, water, lemon juice and zest. Adjust the amount of lemon to your taste. Whip the mixture until it is a light, creamy consistency.

2. Stir the dill into the mixture, again adjusting for taste.

3. Slice the bagels in half. (You can lightly toast the bagels for a lovely crunchy texture, if desired.)

4. Apply the cream cheese generously and top with the smoked salmon and rocket.

Something sweet

'Life is uncertain. Eat dessert first.'
— Ernestine Ulmer

It's all about the little things in life, correct? Enjoying
something sweet is one of those blissful moments.
Whether you have a particular penchant for a perfectly
cooked scone sweetened with homemade strawberry jam
and a dollop of cream; or you love nothing more than
to gather around with loved ones as they delight at the
amazing chocolate cake you've made for dessert, you
should always leave room for a little indulgence.

Baked rice custard

'I used to make this for my three daughters and then I started making it for my five granddaughters and five grandsons — they all love it and request it whenever they come over to my place.' Patricia Smith

SERVES: 4–6

2 cups milk
2 egg yolks
300 ml cream
1½ cups cooked rice, rinsed,
   drained

½ cup caster sugar
½ teaspoon cinnamon
1 teaspoon vanilla extract
pinch of nutmeg, plus extra to
   sprinkle

1. Preheat the oven to 180°C.

2. Combine the milk, egg yolks, cream, rice, sugar, cinnamon, vanilla and nutmeg in a bowl.

3. Pour the mixture into a ceramic ovenproof dish. Stand the dish in a baking dish with enough water to come halfway up the sides. Bake in the oven for 40 minutes, or until the custard is set.

4. Remove from the oven and set aside for 10 minutes before serving. Serve warm.

Grandma's never-fail sponge cake

'I've been making this for many years. It's easy to make and I just whip some cream for the top and add strawberries or flaked chocolate. Kids and adults all eat this and there's never any left.' Dot Livermore

MAKES: TWO CAKES

4 large eggs, separated
¾ cup caster sugar
¾ cup cornflour
¼ cup custard powder
I teaspoon cream of tartar
½ teaspoon bicarbonate of soda

whipped cream, to decorate
strawberries, halved, to
  decorate
30 g Cadbury Flake chocolate
  bar, crumbled, to decorate

1. Preheat the oven to 180°C. Grease two 20 cm round cake tins and line with baking paper.

2. Using an electric mixer, beat the egg whites in a large bowl until soft peaks form. Gradually add the caster sugar, beating to incorporate.

3. Add the egg yolks and beat on medium speed for 5 minutes.

4. Sift the dry ingredients and fold into the mixture.

5. Pour the mixture into the prepared cake tins. Bake for 20 minutes, or until the sponges spring back when lightly touched. Leave to cool in the cake tins for 5 minutes before transferring to a wire rack, top-side up, to cool completely.

6. Once cooled, top with the whipped cream, strawberries and crumbled chocolate.

   Note: Instead of having two cakes, you can sandwich the sponges together with cream and strawberries in the middle.

Rock cakes

Marje Hall

MAKES: 15

115 g unsalted butter, chopped
¼ cup caster sugar
1 egg, beaten
1 cup plain flour
½ cup dates

½ cup sultanas
½ cup walnuts, chopped
¼ teaspoon bicarbonate of
    soda, dissolved in ½ teaspoon
    boiling water

1. Preheat the oven to 180°C. Grease a large baking tray.

2. Using an electric mixer, cream the butter and sugar in a
   bowl. Add the beaten egg and mix. Add the flour and mix.
   Fold in the fruit, nuts and bicarbonate of soda mixture.

3. Place 1½ tablespoons of the mixture on the prepared baking
   tray, leaving room for spreading. Bake for 15–20 minutes, or
   until golden brown. Cool on a wire rack.

Coconut and jam slice

Come afternoon-tea time, nothing will compare to this timeless baked slice. It's a guaranteed crowd-pleaser!

Serves: 15

100 g unsalted butter, softened

¾ cup caster sugar

3 eggs

¾ cup plain flour

½ cup self-raising flour

4 tablespoons buttermilk

⅔ cup raspberry jam

1 cup desiccated coconut

¾ cup shredded coconut

1. Preheat the oven to 180°C. Grease a 3 cm deep, 20 cm x 30 cm slice tin. Line with baking paper, allowing a 2 cm overhang on all sides.

2. Using an electric mixer, beat the butter and ½ cup caster sugar until light and fluffy. Add 1 egg. Beat until combined. Sift the flours into the mixture. Stir to combine. Stir in the buttermilk.

3. Press the mixture into the base of the prepared tin. Spread the raspberry jam over the mixture.

4. Whisk the remaining eggs and caster sugar together in a bowl. Stir in the coconut. Sprinkle the mixture over the jam. Bake for 35–40 minutes, or until lightly golden. Leave to cool in the tin. Cut into pieces to serve.

Cream cheese slice

'I was given this recipe a long time ago. Then I passed it on to my sister, and she has also passed it on. My son also makes this slice and they call it Carol's slice!' Carol Stumbles

SERVES: 10

200 g packet lattice biscuits
3 teaspoons gelatine
½ cup water
250 g cream cheese, chopped
250 g unsalted butter, chopped

1 cup caster sugar
½ teaspoon vanilla extract
whipped cream, to serve
strawberries, halved, to
  decorate

1. Line the base and sides of a Swiss roll tin with baking paper. Place a layer of biscuits, shiny side down, in the base of the tin.

2. Dissolve the gelatine in the water. Pour into a mixing bowl. Add the cream cheese, butter, sugar and vanilla and, using an electric mixer, beat until smooth and creamy.

3. Pour the mixture over the biscuit base. Refrigerate until set.

4. Top with the whipped cream and strawberries (or kiwifruit or grated chocolate). Cut into squares to serve.

Note: Use low-fat cream cheese and whipped cream for fewer calories.

Chocolate coconut meringue torte

'My two sisters and I have been making this recipe since I first came across it in the 80s. Every time I have served it, people just love it. So much so that in fact it is now a dinner party staple that my five daughters make and serve to their friends. It is quite easy and really delicious.' Cheryl O'Brien

SERVES: 8–10

8 egg whites

2 cups caster sugar

2 cups desiccated coconut

120 g unsweetened cocoa powder

I teaspoon vanilla extract or essence

whipped cream, to decorate

strawberries, halved, to decorate (optional)

30 g Cadbury Flake chocolate bar, crumbled, to decorate (optional)

1. Preheat the oven to 180°C. Grease and line the base of a 20 cm springform cake tin with baking paper.

2. Using an electric mixer, beat the egg whites in a clean, dry bowl until firm peaks form. Gradually add the sugar and beat for a few minutes until the sugar has dissolved and the mixture is shiny.

3. Combine the desiccated coconut, cocoa and vanilla in a small bowl. Gently fold into the meringue using a spatula.

4. Spoon into the prepared tin and smooth the surface. Bake for 25–35 minutes, or until the top is set and it is well cooked along the edge. Turn the oven off and leave to cool in the oven (the torte will drop and firm a little as it cools).

5. Carefully transfer the torte to a serving platter. Spoon the whipped cream over the top of the torte. Top with the strawberries and crumbled Flake, if desired.

Fudge

'This was my nana's recipe. Every time we went to Nana's house there was always a tray of fudge in the fridge for us — it was our favourite.' Ruby Carter

MAKES: A BAKING TRAY OF FUDGE

125 g unsalted butter, plus extra
  if needed
½ cup caster sugar
2 tablespoons unsweetened
  cocoa powder
2 eggs, beaten

1 teaspoon vanilla extract
½ cup sultanas
250 g packet plain sweet
  biscuits, crushed
ready-made chocolate icing, to
  decorate

1. Add the butter, sugar and cocoa to a saucepan and bring to the boil over medium heat. Remove the saucepan from the heat and set aside to cool.

2. Stir through the eggs, vanilla and sultanas. Mix in the crushed biscuits.

3. Lightly grease a baking tray. Spoon the mixture onto the tray and smooth the surface using a spatula.

4. Spread the chocolate icing over the top. Refrigerate overnight. Cut into squares to serve.

Easy fruitcake

*'I have been making this cake for more than forty years as it is one
of the easiest, most moist and tastiest cakes to make for special
occasions or to have on hand for visitors. The recipe came from a
collection of recipes put together by the Heathmont East School
Parents Club to sell and raise funds for the school.' Jan Newgreen*

SERVES: 20

1 kg mixed dried fruit

2 cups soft brown sugar

¾ cup sherry or fruit juice

½ cup milk

250 g unsalted butter

3 eggs, beaten

3 cups plain flour

½ teaspoon nutmeg

½ teaspoon cinnamon

½ teaspoon salt

½ teaspoon bicarbonate of soda

1. Combine the fruit, sugar and sherry or juice in a large bowl,
    cover with plastic wrap and leave to stand overnight.

2. Preheat the oven to 150°C. Line the base and sides of a deep
    20 cm round cake tin with baking paper.

3. Heat the milk in a saucepan over medium heat. When warm,
    add the butter, stirring until melted. Add the mixture to the
    prepared fruit mixture.

4. Add the beaten eggs and mix well to combine.

5. Sift the flour and spices together and add to the fruit
    mixture. Add the salt and bicarbonate of soda and stir well.

6. Bake for 2 hours 45 minutes, or until a skewer inserted into the centre comes out clean. Leave to cool in the tin before turning out onto a wire rack to cool completely.

Tip 1: Sprinkle the top with flaked almonds before cooking, if desired.

Tip 2: Place a piece of baking paper on top of the cake to prevent the top from burning, then remove to brown for the last part of the cooking time.

Melted butter biscuits

'In the 1950s, the local Baptist church had each member submit a recipe for their 21st anniversary. This recipe was given by an 80-year-old member, who had it passed to her by her mother. As a mere male, these biscuits are so easy to make. I don't know how long I've been making them … years.' George Hyman

MAKES: 36

1 egg
1 cup caster sugar
200 g unsalted butter, melted

1 teaspoon vanilla extract
2½ cups self-raising flour

1. Preheat the oven to 180°C. Line two baking trays with baking paper.

2. Using an electric mixer, beat the egg and sugar in a large bowl until combined.

3. Add the melted butter and vanilla extract and mix until combined. Slowly add the flour and mix until just combined.

4. Using 2 teaspoons of dough at a time, roll the dough into balls. Place on the prepared baking trays, leaving room for spreading.

5. Bake for about 15 minutes, or until lightly golden.

    Variation: You can also add mixed dried fruit, shredded coconut, chopped nuts or cocoa powder.

Lumberjack cake

Sophie

SERVES: 8

2 apples, peeled, cored, chopped
185 g dates, chopped
1 teaspoon bicarbonate of soda
1 cup boiling water
125 g unsalted butter, chopped
1 cup caster sugar
1 large egg

1 teaspoon vanilla extract
1½ cups plain flour
½ teaspoon salt

Topping
½ cup soft brown sugar
60 g unsalted butter
4 tablespoons milk
60 g shredded coconut

1. Preheat the oven to 180°C. Grease and line a 20 cm round cake tin.

2. Combine the apple and dates in a bowl, add the bicarbonate of soda, pour over the boiling water and leave for about 10 minutes.

3. In a separate bowl, using an electric mixer, beat the butter, sugar, egg and vanilla until light and fluffy.

4. Slowly add the apple and date mixture. Slowly sift in the flour and salt and fold through.

5. Pour into the cake tin and bake for 45–50 minutes, or until a skewer inserted into the centre comes out clean.

The Way Mum Made It

6. To make the topping, combine the sugar, butter and milk in a saucepan over medium heat. Stir until the sugar dissolves. Add the coconut and stir for a further 1–2 minutes.

7. Remove the cake from the oven and evenly spoon the topping over the cake. Return to the oven for a further 15–20 minutes. Leave to cool in the tin for 10 minutes, then transfer to a wire rack to cool completely.

Note: The cake can be served warm or at room temperature with cream, if desired.

Apple turnovers

Delightful to taste and crunchy and soft in texture, classic apple turnovers are actually really quite simple to make.

MAKES: 12

1 kg packet puff pastry sheets
4 apples, peeled, cored, and
　diced
1 tablespoon lemon juice
1 cup soft brown sugar
2 tablespoons cornflour

2½ teaspoons cinnamon
¼ teaspoon nutmeg
1 tablespoon unsalted butter,
　melted
pinch of salt
1 egg, lightly beaten

1. Preheat the oven to 200°C. Line two baking trays with baking paper.

2. Cut the pastry sheets into four equal squares and keep chilled until ready for use.

3. Mix the diced apple with the lemon juice to prevent browning.

4. Add the sugar, cornflour, cinnamon, nutmeg, melted butter and a pinch of salt and mix to combine.

5. Brush the edges of the pastry squares with the lightly beaten egg.

6. Place ⅓ cup of the apple mixture on half of each square and fold the pastry diagonally in half to form a triangle. Seal the turnover by pressing the edges with a fork.

7. Brush the top with more egg wash, and make a small slit to let steam escape. Place on the prepared baking trays.

8. Bake for 20 minutes, or until the pastry is puffed and golden. Serve warm with cream or ice cream, or at room temperature.

Apricot loaf

Emily Wadham

SERVES: 10

I cup All-Bran
½ cup caster sugar
I cup milk
I cup self-raising flour

I cup chopped dried apricots
I tablespoon golden syrup
2 tablespoons desiccated
   coconut

1. Preheat the oven to 180°C. Lightly grease a loaf tin.

2. Combine the All-Bran, caster sugar and milk in a bowl and
   set aside for at least 30 minutes.

3. Add the self-raising flour, dried apricots and golden syrup
   to the All-Bran mixture and mix well.

4. Spoon the mixture into the loaf tin and sprinkle with the
   desiccated coconut.

5. Bake for 45 minutes, or until a skewer inserted into
   the centre comes out clean. Leave to cool in the tin for
   5 minutes, then turn out onto a wire rack to cool completely.
   Serve sliced, with butter.

The perfect scones

There's nothing finer in life than freshly baked scones with jam and cream served with a cup of tea. Here's everything you need to know to make a perfect batch.

SERVES: 16

3 cups self-raising flour
40 g chilled butter, chopped
2 teaspoons caster sugar
pinch of salt

1½ cups buttermilk, plus extra
   to glaze
raspberry jam, to serve
thick cream, to serve

1. Preheat the oven to 230°C. Lightly dust a square cake tin with flour.

2. Sift the flour into a large bowl. Using your fingertips, rub the butter into the flour until it resembles breadcrumbs. Add the sugar and salt. Make a well in the centre and pour the buttermilk into it. Using a knife in a cutting motion, stir the mixture until a soft dough forms. You may need to add more buttermilk to soften the dough.

3. Turn the dough out onto a lightly floured work surface. Knead until the dough just comes together. Be gentle and make sure you don't overwork it — this is what causes tough scones. Using your fingertips, gently pat the dough into a disc about 3 cm thick.

4. Using a 5 cm diameter round cutter dipped in flour, cut the scones from the dough. Re-use any excess dough. Arrange the scones in the prepared tin so they are only just touching. Lightly brush the tops with the extra buttermilk.

5. Bake on the top shelf of the oven for 10–12 minutes, or until golden and the scones sound hollow when tapped. Serve warm with jam and cream.

Banana bread

'I have been making this for 40 years and my hubby still requests it. If I try a new cake, he says "What's wrong with the banana cake? I like it!"' Marilyn Hulslander

SERVES: 8–10

125 g unsalted butter, chopped
I cup caster sugar
I teaspoon vanilla extract
2 large eggs

¾ cup mashed ripe bananas (about 2)
I¼ cups self-raising flour
¾ teaspoon bicarbonate of soda
I teaspoon salt

1. Preheat the oven to 180°C. Lightly grease and flour a loaf tin.

2. Using an electric mixer, beat the butter and sugar thoroughly, adding the vanilla while mixing.

3. Add the eggs, one at a time, beating thoroughly after each addition. Add the banana and beat on low speed.

4. In a separate bowl, combine the flour, bicarbonate of soda and salt and add to the banana mixture. Continue mixing on low speed until combined, then mix on medium speed for 2 minutes.

5. Pour into the prepared tin and bake for 45 minutes. Leave to cool in the tin for 5 minutes, then cut around the sides and turn out onto a wire rack to cool.

Note: This basic recipe can be enhanced by adding ½ cup of chopped walnuts, shaken with a little bit of flour, and stirred into the mixture after you've finished beating. You can also add a teaspoon of ground ginger if you like.

Apple pie

There's nothing quite like a warm slice of apple pie. Served with ice cream. Or cream. Or custard. Or all three, if you're feeling especially naughty. This recipe combines homemade pastry with an irresistible filling for a classic dessert that won't last long in your fridge.

SERVES: 8–10

Pastry

1¾ cups plain flour

½ cup self-raising flour

pinch of salt

185 g unsalted butter, chilled and cut into small cubes

⅓ cup caster sugar, plus 1 tablespoon extra, to sprinkle

2 eggs

1 tablespoon chilled water

1 tablespoon milk

Filling

1.1 kg apples (we like to use a mixture of granny smith and golden delicious), peeled, cored, sliced about 5 mm thick

¼ cup sugar

¼ cup soft brown sugar

1 tablespoon lemon juice

1 teaspoon cinnamon

¼ teaspoon nutmeg

¼ teaspoon salt

2 tablespoons unsalted butter

1½ tablespoons cornflour

1. To make the pastry, sift the flours and salt into a large mixing bowl. Rub the butter lightly through the flour using your fingertips. When the mixture resembles fine breadcrumbs, stir through ⅓ cup of sugar.

2. Lightly beat 1 egg with the chilled water. Cut this mixture into the flour mixture using a butter knife to bring the dough together.

3. Form the dough into a ball (add a little more water if necessary). Divide into two pieces, one slightly larger. Wrap in plastic wrap and refrigerate for 30 minutes.

4. To make the filling, combine the apple slices with the sugars, lemon juice, cinnamon, nutmeg, and salt in a large bowl. Leave this to sit at room temperature for 30 minutes–3 hours.

5. Tip the apples into a strainer set over a large bowl (to capture the juices). Leave this to drain for up to 30 minutes. You should have about ½ cup of juice.

6. Pour the juices into a small saucepan with the unsalted butter and boil over medium heat until the mixture reduces to about ⅓ cup. Mix the apple slices with the cornflour and then toss with the reduced apple syrup.

7. Roll out the bigger pastry ball to form a 30 cm circle (2 mm thick). Transfer the pastry to a 22 cm pie dish. Gently press the pastry into the corners and allow any excess to hang over the edge.

8. Roll out the smaller ball of pastry to form a 25 cm circle.

9. Pour the apple mixture into the pie dish.

10. Mix the remaining egg with the milk and brush a little of this mixture onto the edge of the piecrust. Cover the apple mixture with the remaining pastry top.

11. Trim any excess pastry, and crimp the edges with your fingers. Chill the pie in the fridge for 30 minutes.

12. Preheat the oven to 200°C. Brush the pie with more of the beaten egg and milk. Sprinkle the remaining caster sugar over the top. Cut four small air vents in the pie and bake for 45 minutes, or until lightly golden.

Vanilla custard squares

Lyn

SERVES: 8

2 sheets puff pastry
600 ml cream

2 x 100 g packets instant vanilla
    pudding mix
1 cup milk

1. Preheat the oven to 210°C. Line a 23 cm square cake tin
    with foil, making sure that the foil comes up over the sides
    (this allows you to lift out the slice).

2. Place each pastry sheet on a baking tray lined with baking
    paper. Bake for 8–10 minutes, or until lightly golden. Set
    aside to cool. Once cool, place 1 pastry sheet, cooked-side
    up, in the bottom of the tin. (You may need to trim it
    slightly to fit.)

3. Using an electric mixer, beat the cream, pudding mix and
    milk in a bowl. Pour over the pastry sheet in the tin. Place
    the remaining pastry sheet on top. Refrigerate overnight.

4. Remove from the tin, cut into squares and serve.

    Note: You can top with vanilla icing if you like.

Plum cake

*This delicious plum cake is complete with a crumbly
golden crust and beautifully tender juicy plums. It's
the perfect morning or afternoon treat.*

SERVES: 8

9 black plums (tinned are fine)
115 g unsalted butter
½ cup caster sugar
2 eggs, separated

1 tablespoon milk
170 g plain flour
1 teaspoon baking powder
icing sugar, for sprinkling

1. Preheat the oven to 180°C. Grease a 20 cm round cake tin.

2. Cut the plums open and drain on paper towels.

3. Using an electric mixer, cream the butter and sugar together
    until light and fluffy.

4. Beat the egg yolks lightly, then add along with the milk
    and mix well. Sift in the flour and baking powder and fold
    together.

5. Beat the egg whites in a separate bowl until soft peaks form.
    Fold into the mixture lightly with a knife.

6. Spoon the batter into the prepared tin. Place the plums on
    top, cut side down.

7. Bake for 55–60 minutes. Remove from the tin, sprinkle
    with the icing sugar and serve warm with cream or ice
    cream.

Gin and tonic cupcakes

We love this adults-only treat that's deliciously fresh and very sophisticated. You can leave the gin out, if desired (or substitute it for vodka if that's more your style), we just like having these cocktail cakes to serve after dinner, or at a birthday.

MAKES: 12

125 g unsalted butter, at room temperature, chopped

¾ cup caster sugar

3 tablespoons milk

2 tablespoons gin

juice and zest of 1 lime

2 eggs, lightly beaten

1½ cups plain flour, sifted

½ teaspoon salt

½ teaspoon baking powder

1 lime, cut into thin wedges, to serve (optional)

Icing

100 g unsalted butter, at room temperature, chopped

2¼ cups icing sugar, sifted

2 tablespoons gin

1–2 tablespoons lime juice

1. Preheat the oven to 180°C. Line a 12-hole muffin tin with paper cases.

2. Using an electric mixer, beat the butter and sugar until light and fluffy.

3. Reduce the speed of the mixer and add the milk, gin and lime juice and zest. Add half of the beaten egg and mix until just incorporated. Mix in the remaining egg and beat for a further 1–2 minutes.

The Way Mum Made It

4. Using a large spatula, gently fold in the flour, salt and baking powder until the batter is just combined.

5. Spoon the batter into the paper cases and bake for 15–20 minutes, or until lightly golden. Leave to cool.

6. To make the icing, beat the butter and sugar until creamy, then add the remaining ingredients and beat on high speed until the icing reaches the desired consistency.

7. Once the cakes have cooled completely, spread or pipe the icing on top. Place a thin wedge of lime on top, if desired, and serve.

Steamed date pudding

*'I still have the handwritten recipe from my late mum, which
was given to her by my dad's sister, my auntie Jean. This
recipe means a lot to me; looking at my mum's handwriting
brings tears to my eyes.' Jennifer Ellen Fildes*

SERVES: 4–6

1½ cups finely chopped dates
1 cup milk
¼ cup caster sugar

2 tablespoons unsalted butter
1 teaspoon bicarbonate of soda
1 cup self-raising flour

1. Combine the dates, milk, sugar and butter in a saucepan and
   bring to the boil over medium heat. Add the bicarbonate of
   soda and while still frothing, add the self-raising flour. Stir
   until combined.

2. Grease an 8 cup capacity metal pudding steamer. Add the
   mixture to the dish. Cover with baking paper, then foil.
   Cover with the lid and secure with rubber bands.

3. Place in a large saucepan. Carefully pour boiling water into
   the saucepan until halfway up the side of the steamer. Cover
   with a lid. Place the saucepan over medium heat and bring to
   the boil. Reduce the heat to low. Simmer for 1 hour, topping
   up with boiling water when necessary.

4. Remove the pan from the heat. Carefully lift the steamer
   from the water. Stand for 10 minutes, then remove the lid.
   Turn the pudding out onto a plate. Serve with cream and or
   custard.

Apple and cinnamon teacake

*Sure to delight every time, this light and delicious
teacake is suitable for any occasion.*

SERVES: 8–10

80 g unsalted butter, at room
   temperature
½ cup caster sugar
I egg
I teaspoon vanilla extract
I cup self-raising flour

½ teaspoon cinnamon
½ cup milk
2 small red apples, quartered,
   cored and cut into thin slices
20 g unsalted butter, melted
I tablespoon demerara sugar

I.   Preheat the oven to 180°C. Grease a 20 cm springform cake
     tin and line the base with baking paper.

2.   Using an electric mixer, beat the butter and caster
     sugar until light and creamy. Add the egg and beat until
     combined, then beat in the vanilla.

3.   Sift the flour and cinnamon over the butter mixture and add
     the milk. Using a spatula, fold together until just combined,
     taking care not to overbeat.

4.   Pour the batter into the prepared tin, making sure it is
     spread evenly. Smooth the surface.

5. Arrange the apple slices in a circular pattern on top of the batter.

6. Bake for 35–40 minutes, or until golden brown. Brush the warm cake with the melted butter and sprinkle with the demerara sugar.

Cockles biscuits

'I am in my late 70s and this recipe has been passed down from my mother and possibly my grandmother. It has always been a favourite of all the family.' Lynette Royal

MAKES: 30

180 g unsalted butter, at room
  temperature
180 g caster sugar
3 eggs
½ teaspoon vanilla extract

180 g plain flour
180 g cornflour
1 teaspoon cream of tartar
½ teaspoon bicarbonate of soda
raspberry jam

1. Preheat the oven to 160°C. Line a baking tray with baking paper.

2. Using an electric mixer, cream the butter and sugar. Add the eggs, one at a time, until combined. Add the vanilla and mix.

3. Sift the flours with the cream of tartar and bicarbonate of soda twice. Carefully fold the flours into the butter mixture.

4. Place small teaspoons of the mixture onto the prepared tray, leaving room for spreading. Bake for 12–15 minutes. Leave to cool.

5. When cool, join two cockles together with the raspberry jam.

Dutch honey cake

'I used to make this cake when my children were small and I still do. Everybody loves it, including me. My husband is Dutch but it is not one of his family recipes.' Dorothy Karman

SERVES: 10–12

2½ cups self-raising flour
1 cup soft brown sugar
1 tablespoon honey
1 teaspoon cinnamon

½ teaspoon ground cloves
½ teaspoon nutmeg
¾ cup milk

1. Preheat the oven to 180°C. Grease and flour a loaf tin.

2. Combine all of the ingredients in a large bowl. Pour the mixture into the prepared tin.

3. Bake for 45–55 minutes, or until a skewer inserted into the centre comes out clean. Leave to cool in the tin for 5 minutes before turning out onto a wire rack to cool completely.

4. When cool, slice and serve buttered.

The Way Mum Made It

Choc self-saucing pudding

'My late mother used to make this and it was a family favourite. When my son became a chef he asked for the recipe to use at the Adelaide Crows Football Club restaurant. It was there for many years. Sadly Mum was not alive when my children were born, but she would have been very surprised, and probably a little bit thrilled, that they always asked for Grandma's chocolate pudding on their birthdays.' Dee Vawser

SERVES: 8

1 cup self-raising flour
1½ tablespoons unsweetened
  cocoa powder
1½ tablespoons soft brown
  sugar
¾ cup milk
2 tablespoons unsalted butter,
  melted

1 teaspoon vanilla extract
icing sugar, for dusting
ice cream, to serve
Sauce
1½ cups boiling water
1½ tablespoons unsweetened
  cocoa powder
¾ cup soft brown sugar

1. Preheat the oven to 180°C. Grease a 1.5 litre (6 cup) capacity ovenproof baking dish.

2. Sift the flour and cocoa together in a large bowl. Add the brown sugar, milk, melted butter and vanilla. Mix well. Pour the mixture into the prepared dish.

3. To make the sauce, mix together the boiling water, cocoa and sugar and gently pour over the pudding mix.

4. Bake for 30 minutes. Dust with the icing sugar and serve warm with ice cream.

Apple and caramel
upside-down cake

*Refreshing and juicy, yet with a little crunch and decadence, this
spin on the classic upside-down cake will wow your guests.*

SERVES: 8–10

5 royal gala apples, cored, each
   cut into 6 wedges
2¼ cups caster sugar
¾ cup water
300 g unsalted butter, softened
1½ teaspoons vanilla extract
2 cups plain flour
1 tablespoon baking powder
75 g ground almonds

1 teaspoon ground cardamom
½ teaspoon salt
7 eggs, at room temperature
4 tablespoons milk
thick cream, to serve
Strawberry sauce
2 x 380 g jars strawberry jam
1½ cups water

1. Preheat the oven to 170°C. Grease and line the base of a
   25 cm springform cake tin.

2. Starting from the edge of the tin, tightly pack the apple
   wedges, skin-side down, in a ring, then pack the remaining
   wedges into the centre. Remove the wedges from the tin,
   re-creating the formation on a work surface.

3. Place 1 cup of the sugar and the water in a small, heavy-
   based saucepan and stir over medium heat until the sugar
   dissolves. Bring to the boil, then simmer to a dark caramel.

4. Pour the caramel into the prepared tin, pouring around the edge first, then in the centre. Working quickly, carefully arrange the apple wedges over the caramel.

5. Using an electric mixer, beat the butter, vanilla and remaining sugar until pale and fluffy.

6. Sift the flour, baking powder, almonds, cardamom and salt into the butter mixture. Add the eggs and milk and beat on low speed until smooth and combined. Spoon the batter over the apple wedges and smooth the surface.

7. Place the tin on the bottom shelf of the oven for 30 minutes, then cover with baking paper to prevent over-browning. Bake for a further 45 minutes, or until a skewer inserted into the centre comes out clean. Cool in the tin for 15 minutes, then run a knife around the side of the cake and turn out onto a plate.

8. To make the strawberry sauce, place the jam and water in a small saucepan over medium heat and simmer for 5 minutes, or until smooth.

9. Serve the upside-down cake warm or at room temperature with the cream and strawberry sauce drizzled over.

   Note: The strawberry sauce makes 2¼ cups. It will keep in an airtight container in the fridge for up to two weeks.

Meringue sago pudding

'This recipe was passed on from an old aunt who lived her whole life on a dairy farm. It is very simple but an absolute hit with everyone, you can even convert those who don't like sago.' Elizabeth Wilson

SERVES: 4–6

2½ cups milk
3 tablespoons washed sago
140 g caster sugar

2 eggs, separated
½ cup shredded coconut

1. Bring the milk to the boil in a saucepan over medium heat. Add the washed sago along with 3 tablespoons of the caster sugar. Simmer until the sago is cooked and becomes translucent, stirring constantly as the sugar can catch on the bottom of the pan. Remove from the stovetop.

2. Beat the eggs yolks and add to the mixture. Return to the stove until the mixture thickens. Place in an ovenproof dish. Preheat the oven to 180°C.

3. Using an electric mixer, beat the egg whites until stiff peaks form. Gradually add in the remaining sugar. Spread on top of the sago and sprinkle the coconut on top.

4. Bake until the meringue has browned. Serve warm with cream or ice cream.

Lemon and butter almond slice

Beverley Quigley

SERVES: 16

250 g unsalted butter, softened, chopped
2 teaspoons vanilla extract
1¼ cups caster sugar
⅔ cup ground almonds
2 cups plain flour
2 cups flaked almonds
icing sugar, for dusting

Lemon butter
1 teaspoon grated lemon zest
⅔ cup strained fresh lemon juice
1½ cups caster sugar
250 g unsalted butter, chopped
4 eggs, beaten lightly, strained

1. To make the lemon butter, combine the zest, juice, sugar, butter and eggs in a medium-sized heavy-based saucepan. Heat over very low heat and stir constantly for about 10 minutes, or until thickened. Cover and refrigerate for a few hours, or until thick.

2. Preheat the oven to 200°C. Grease a baking tin and line the base and two opposite sides with baking paper, making sure the paper extends a few centimetres above the edges.

3. Using an electric mixer, beat the butter, vanilla extract and sugar in a bowl until light and fluffy. Transfer to large bowl and add the ground almonds and sifted flour, gently folding to combine.

4. Press two-thirds of the pastry evenly over the base of the prepared tin. Wrap the remaining pastry in plastic wrap and refrigerate.

5. Bake the base, uncovered, for about 12 minutes, or until browned lightly. Leave to cool for 10 minutes.

6. Spread the base with the lemon butter. Crumble the reserved pastry on top and sprinkle with the flaked almonds.

7. Bake the slice for 25 minutes, or until lightly golden. Leave to cool in the tin, then remove, dust with the sifted icing sugar and cut into pieces.

Coconut and apricot cake

'The easiest cake ever that anyone can make.' Anna Woltschenko

SERVES: 8–10

1 cup self-raising flour
1 cup caster sugar
1 cup shredded coconut

1 cup chopped dried apricots
1 cup milk

1. Preheat the oven to 180°C. Grease a loaf tin and line with baking paper.

2. Combine all of the dried ingredients in a large bowl. Add the milk and mix well.

3. Pour the mixture into the prepared tin.

4. Bake for 40–45 minutes, or until a skewer inserted into the centre comes out clean. Cut into slices to serve.

Note: Suitable for vegans and coeliacs if you use gluten-free flour, rapadura sugar and almond or coconut milk.

Steamed golden sponge pudding

'I was given this recipe by a late friend and have used it for nearly 50 years. It's my friends' and family's favourite and inexpensive to make.' Barb Walker

SERVES: 4–6

2 tablespoons unsalted butter
2 tablespoons golden syrup
½ teaspoon bicarbonate of soda

¾ cup milk
1 cup plain flour

1. Melt the butter and golden syrup in a saucepan over low heat. Stir in the bicarbonate of soda and milk. Add the flour, stirring until there are no lumps.

2. Pour the mixture into an ovenproof dish. Cover with a lid and place in a pot of boiling water. Steam for 1 hour.

Note: This is a light, fluffy pudding, which can be served with custard, cream or ice cream.

Carmel's carrot cake

'The recipe has featured at our family gatherings for some 40 years now, and is shamelessly calorific. Known in the family as Carmel's carrot cake, it came to us via an old family friend who told us that it had come into her family via an outback station cook which goes some way, I guess, to explaining its very generous size and the fact that the original recipe suggests that it be cooked in a baking dish. I love a recipe with provenance! Now embraced by a new generation of cooks led by my daughter-in-law, Katie, the cake has featured in her sister's London cafe and more recently at another sister's wedding. For a recent occasion, to put two carrot-averse kids "off the scent" so to speak, I renamed the cake "Gaby's Golden Cake"!' Gabrielle Foster

SERVES: 8–10

2 cups caster sugar

4 eggs

1½ cups light olive oil

2 cups plain flour

2 teaspoons cinnamon

2 teaspoons bicarbonate of soda

pinch of salt

3 cups grated carrot

1 cup chopped walnuts

Icing

375 g icing sugar

150 g unsalted butter, chopped

250 g cream cheese

1 teaspoon vanilla extract

1. Preheat the oven to 180°C. Lightly grease a 24 cm x 40 cm loose-based cake tin.

2. Using an electric mixer, beat the sugar and eggs until creamy. Gradually add the oil while mixing. Fold in the flour sifted with the cinnamon, bicarbonate of soda and salt. Mix through the carrot and walnuts.

3. Pour the mixture into the prepared tin. Bake for 45 minutes, or until a skewer inserted into the centre comes out clean. Leave to cool completely in the tin.

4. To make the icing, use an electric mixer to beat all the ingredients until well combined.

5. Once the cake is cool, spread with the icing and then refrigerate until ready to serve.

   Note: This cake is best made a couple of days in advance to allow the flavours to develop, and will keep in the refrigerator for 7–10 days.

Cooking with kids

*'Food, for me, is the most central theme of everything
I love. It brings people together in the most wonderful
way. Whether you're cooking or just sharing the table,
I wouldn't be without it.'*
— Maggie Beer

If there's one thing that's important to pass onto
children, it's the family secrets from the kitchen.
Whether that is sharing with them recipes that have been
passed down or simply showing little ones how to cook
your favourite meals, instilling in kids the love of home-
style cooking is something they will be able to delight in
for years to come. It's also a great way to create lasting
memories with them that they will hold on to their
entire lives. Plus, cooking with kids is a lot of fun!

Chocolate crackles

The grandkids will love these chocolate crackles as much as they will enjoy you teaching them how to make them. In fact, most adults will enjoy these old favourites too.

MAKES: 24

4 cups Rice Bubbles
1 cup icing sugar
1 cup desiccated coconut

100 g unsweetened cocoa
powder
250 g Copha, melted

1. In a large bowl, mix the Rice Bubbles, icing sugar, coconut and cocoa using a wooden spoon.

2. In a saucepan over low heat, slowly melt the Copha. Allow to cool slightly. Add to the Rice Bubble mixture, stirring until well combined.

3. Spoon the mixture evenly into 24 paper patty cases and refrigerate until firm.

Lemon cordial

Rosie Kennett

MAKES: 1.5 LITRES

2.25 kg caster sugar
1.7 litres water
3 tablespoons tartaric acid

1½ tablespoons citric acid
1½ tablespoons Epsom salt
juice and zest of 8 large lemons

1. Add the sugar and water to a large saucepan and bring to the boil over medium heat. Boil for 5 minutes, then remove from the heat.

2. Add the tartaric acid, citric acid and Epsom salt. Stir to dissolve and leave to cool.

3. Add the lemon juice and zest. Transfer the mixture to a large jug to serve.

Parmesan-crusted baked chicken nuggets

This recipe is great to make if you're having the grandkids over for dinner. In fact, why not get them in the kitchen making this dish themselves?

SERVES: 4

500 g chicken breast fillets
1¼ cups garlic breadcrumbs
⅓ cup grated parmesan cheese
¼ teaspoon salt

1 tablespoon vegetable oil
4 tablespoons plain flour
2 large eggs, lightly beaten

1. Preheat the oven to 200°C. Cut the chicken into nugget-sized pieces.

2. Spread a thin layer of breadcrumbs on a baking tray and bake for 5 minutes, or until lightly golden.

3. Pour the breadcrumbs into a bowl with the parmesan and salt, and mix with the vegetable oil.

4. In small batches, coat the chicken pieces in the flour, shaking off any excess. Then dip in the beaten egg, before coating in the breadcrumbs.

5. Place on a lightly greased wire rack on top of a baking tray in the oven. Bake at 230°C for 10–12 minutes, turning halfway. Serve warm with your favourite dipping sauce.

Note: To make this for one person, divide ingredients by four.

Yoghurt-oil pizza dough

'I started making this dough as an alternative to the pizza dough with yeast. It is easy and tastes delicious. I don't get to see my grandson very often but when I do see him we love to make lots of mini pizzas with all sorts of toppings. Sometimes he would even put sprinkles on it! It is so much fun. Which kid doesn't love to play with dough, not to mention eat pizza?' Petra Engelhardt

MAKES: 2 PORTIONS

125 g plain yoghurt
5 tablespoons olive oil
1 egg
200 g plain flour

1 teaspoon baking powder
1 teaspoon salt
your choice of pizza sauce and
   toppings

1. Preheat the oven to 180°C. Line a baking tray with baking paper.

2. Mix the yoghurt, olive oil and egg in a bowl.

3. Add the flour, baking powder and salt and knead into the dough, until it becomes a thick, non-sticky mass.

4. Take a piece of the dough, turn it out onto a lightly floured surface and roll out.

5. Transfer to the prepared baking tray. Add your choice of sauce and toppings. Bake in the oven for about 15 minutes.

    Note: This pizza base tastes great topped with ham and blue cheese.

Betty's sausage rolls

'I used to visit Mum once every two weeks and we used to cook various meals on the weekend and the one that stood out was her sausage rolls. She has since passed away, but her yummy sausage rolls live on. You won't be able to stop at one.' Lynda Marshall

MAKES: 60–70

1 kg sausage meat
1 zucchini, grated
2 carrots, grated
2 red onions, finely diced
3 garlic cloves, minced

3 slices white bread, made into breadcrumbs
2 packets chicken noodle soup
1 kg packet puff pastry sheets
2–3 tablespoons milk

1. Preheat the oven to 180°C. Line a baking tray with baking paper.

2. In a large bowl, mix the sausage meat, zucchini, carrot, onion, garlic and breadcrumbs.

3. Put the chicken noodle soup in a small bowl and add enough boiling water to cover the soup so the noodles go soft.

4. Add the soup to the sausage mixture and mix well.

5. Cut the pastry sheets in half and arrange the mixture in a long sausage along the length of the pastry. Roll the pastry around the sausage mixture, making sure the edge of the pastry sheet is underneath.

6. Cut the sausage rolls to the desired size and place on the prepared tray. Brush the sausage rolls with milk and bake for approximately 45–50 minutes.

Fish pie

A great meal for the entire family to enjoy — this fish pie is simple to make, so little ones can assist, and yet it's still very satisfying.

SERVES: 6–8

200 g boneless white fish fillets
200 g skinless salmon fillet, pin-boned (ask your fishmonger to do this)
salt and pepper, to season
450 ml milk
750 g desiree potatoes, peeled, chopped

100 g unsalted butter
2 tablespoons plain flour
150 g frozen peas
1 tablespoon flat-leaf parsley leaves, chopped
3 hard-boiled eggs, chopped
juice of ½ lemon
50 g cheddar cheese, grated

1. Preheat the oven to 170°C.

2. Place the fish in a baking dish, season with salt and pepper and pour over 400 ml of the milk. Cover with foil and bake for 15 minutes, or until the fish flakes away slightly when pressed with a fork. Remove the fish, reserving the milk. When cool enough to handle, flake the fish into bite-sized pieces.

3. Cook the potatoes in boiling salted water until tender. Drain and keep warm.

4. Melt half the butter in a saucepan, stir in the flour and cook over low heat for 2–3 minutes. Slowly add the reserved milk to the roux and continue to cook until thickened. Add the fish, peas, parsley, egg and lemon juice and season with salt and pepper.

5. Mash the potato with the remaining 50 ml of milk and the remaining butter until smooth, then season.

6. Pile the fish mixture into a 1 litre capacity baking dish, spoon the potato mash on top and smooth with a spatula. Sprinkle with the grated cheese and bake for 20–25 minutes, or until golden.

Little molten mud cakes

'Found this recipe in one of the camps I cooked in on the old Ghan line — an old cook left it. Used to be done in a wood oven. I'd make them for the boys in camp and they loved them.' Graham Egan

MAKES: 12

200 g dark chocolate, chopped, plus 120 g extra, cut into 12 squares
200 g unsalted butter, chopped
3 eggs

½ cup caster sugar
1 teaspoon vanilla extract
¾ cup self-raising flour, sifted
unsweetened cocoa powder, for dusting

1. Preheat the oven to 160°C. Line a 12-hole muffin tin with paper cases.

2. Place the chocolate and butter in a saucepan over low heat, stirring, until melted and smooth.

3. Using an electric mixer, beat the eggs, sugar and vanilla for 6–8 minutes, or until pale and doubled in volume.

4. Add the chocolate mixture and flour and fold until well combined.

The Way Mum Made It

5. Divide the mixture between the paper cases. Push 1 piece of the extra chocolate into the middle of each cake and smooth the surfaces. Bake for 30–35 minutes, or until the cakes feel firm to the touch.

6. Allow to cool in the tin for 5 minutes before transferring to wire racks until just warm. Dust with the cocoa to serve.

Baked fish fingers

From grandkids to grandparents, who doesn't like good old fish fingers?
With fresh herbs and a healthy spin you can enjoy these guilt free.

SERVES: 6–8

¼ cup plain flour

2 eggs

2 cups cornflakes, crushed

3 tablespoon finely chopped
   dill

½ teaspoon salt

400 g cod

oil spray

½ cup fat-free Greek yoghurt

2 tablespoons finely chopped
   dill pickles

lemon wedges, to serve

1. Preheat the oven to 220°C. Line a baking tray with baking paper.

2. Add the flour to a shallow bowl. Place the eggs in a separate bowl and whisk. Combine the cornflakes, 1 teaspoon of dill and the salt in a third shallow bowl.

3. Pat the fish dry with paper towels. Cut into long sticks (about 15 pieces). Dip each piece first in the flour, then coat with the egg, then dip in the cornflake mixture. Lay the fish pieces on the baking tray. Lightly spray with the oil.

4. Bake in the centre of the oven for 10 minutes, or until golden brown, flipping halfway through.

5. Meanwhile, combine the yoghurt with the pickles and the remaining dill in a small dipping bowl. Serve alongside the fish fingers with the lemon wedges.

The Way Mum Made It

Gluten-free orange cake

Anne Taylor

SERVES: 6

250 g oranges (see note)   250 g ground almonds
6 eggs   1 teaspoon baking powder
250 g caster sugar

1. Place the whole oranges in a saucepan of water, cover and simmer gently for 2 hours. Set aside to cool.

2. Preheat the oven to 180°C. Grease and flour a 20 cm springform cake tin.

3. Cut the oranges into quarters and remove the seeds. Purée the oranges, together with the skin, in a food processor. Measure out 250 g of the pulp. (This step is essential so the cake is not too mushy and will set.)

3. Beat the eggs and sugar until thick and pale. Fold in the ground almonds, baking powder and orange pulp.

4. Pour into the tin and bake for 30–40 minutes, or until a skewer inserted into the centre comes out clean. Leave to cool in the tin.

5. If desired, serve with orange slices, marinated in Cointreau, with cream cheese icing.

   Note: I cook four to five oranges at a time and measure out 250 g lots and put the extra in the freezer for the next cake. You will make this cake time and time again and this saves cooking oranges each time.

The Way Mum Made It

Shortbread

'I have fond memories of cooking with my mum (who is now deceased) as a child and her favourite recipe was shortbread. I remember her letting me mix the ingredients with my little hands. It was so lovely to come home from school and smell the homemade goodies. This shortbread is so delicious and my mum had a special order once she had grandchildren because they wanted it for their school lunchboxes. I am now a nana and make it for my grandchildren. I am thankful to my mum for teaching me to cook.' Heather Self

SERVES: 10

115 g unsalted butter, at room
   temperature
55 g caster sugar

2 drops vanilla extract
175 g plain flour

1. Preheat the oven to 150°C. Grease a 20 cm round or square tin.

2. Combine the butter, sugar and vanilla in a bowl and beat until soft.

3. Mix in the flour and fold to combine.

4. Pour the mixture into the prepared tin and smooth the surface.

5. Prick all over with a fork and make 10 score lines around the shortbread. Place in the oven and bake for 1 hour, or until pale golden in colour and firm to the touch.

6. Place on a wire rack to cool.

Macaroni and cheese

A quick family dinner that everyone will love, this macaroni cheese is easy to make and will not disappoint — especially the grandkids.

SERVES: 4–6

350 g macaroni pasta
50 g butter, plus a little extra
   for greasing
50 g plain flour
700 ml milk

175 g mature cheddar cheese,
   grated
50 g parmesan cheese, grated
50 g coarse white breadcrumbs

1. Preheat the oven to 200°C. Cook the pasta in a large saucepan of boiling salted water until just tender. Drain well.

2. Melt the butter in a saucepan over medium heat. When foaming, add the flour, then cook, stirring constantly, for 1 minute over low heat. Remove the saucepan from the heat. Whisk in the milk. Return to medium heat. Cook, stirring constantly, until the sauce boils and thickens. Stir in the cheddar cheese.

3. Lightly grease an ovenproof dish. Stir the cooked macaroni into the cheese sauce. Spoon into the dish. Sprinkle the parmesan and breadcrumbs over the top.

4. Bake for 15–20 minutes, or until golden brown and bubbling. Serve with a salad, if desired.

   Note: To make this dish healthier, try gluten-free pasta and low-fat cheese.

Passionfruit pudding

'This was my mother's recipe and was a regular for dessert served with ice cream. It's so easy and now my children and grandchildren love to make it. It's refreshing and great if on a budget.' Judy Coburn

SERVES: 4

1 packet lemon jelly
2 cups boiling water
2 tablespoons caster sugar

2 eggs
1 cup cold milk
pulp of 4 passionfruit

1. In a heatproof bowl, combine the jelly, boiling water and sugar.

2. Beat the eggs and milk together. Add the jelly to the egg mixture.

3. When the mixture has cooled, pour the passionfruit on top and allow to set.

Note: Sugar can be left out if you want to watch your calories.

Salmon fishcakes

Healthy and delicious, these tasty fishcakes will not only be enjoyed by all, but they also store well in the freezer so you can always have a speedy meal on hand if you need.

MAKES: 8

salt and pepper, to season
600 g potatoes, peeled and
  chopped into 1 cm pieces
50 g peas (fresh or frozen)
½ bunch fresh chives, finely
  chopped

2 x 180 g tins salmon, drained
finely grated zest of 1 lemon
1 tablespoon plain flour, plus
  extra for dusting
1 large egg
olive oil

1. Half-fill a large saucepan with cold water and add a tiny pinch of salt. Place over high heat and bring to the boil.

2. Once the water is boiling, carefully add the potatoes, bring back to the boil, then turn the heat down to medium and simmer gently for around 10 minutes, or until cooked through. Add the peas for the last 2 minutes. Once cooked, drain the potatoes and peas and leave them to cool completely.

3. In a mixing bowl, add the chives and salmon. Using a fork, flake into small chunks.

4. Add the lemon zest to the bowl along with the flour. Add the egg and a pinch of pepper.

5. Tip the potatoes and peas back into the pan and use a potato masher to mash. Add the mash to the salmon mixture and mix until well combined.

6. Sprinkle a little flour over a clean work surface and onto a large plate. Divide the salmon mixture into eight portions and use your hands to pat and shape each ball into a fishcake, roughly 2 cm thick. Place on the floured plate, dusting your hands and the top of each fish cake lightly with flour as you go.

7. Heat a large frying pan over medium heat and add 1 tablespoon of olive oil. Carefully place the fishcakes in the pan and cook for 3–4 minutes on each side, or until crisp and golden, turning carefully with a fish slice. Drain on paper towels and keep warm.

Kiss biscuits

'My auntie, Edna McDermott, won first prize at the State Cooking Contest in July 1976 with this kiss biscuit recipe. She handwrote the recipe out for me about 30 years ago and it's still very popular in our family. I am a third-generation member of the Glenorchy Branch of the CWA of Tasmania.' Judith Morris

MAKES: APPROXIMATELY 60

225 g self-raising flour
1 tablespoon cornflour
pinch of salt
110 g margarine (I use half
  unsalted butter and half
  margarine)

115 g sugar
1 egg
1 teaspoon vanilla extract

1. Preheat the oven to 180°C. Line a baking tray with baking paper.

2. Sift the flour, cornflour and salt into a bowl.

3. Using an electric mixer, cream the margarine and sugar. Add the egg and vanilla to the sugar mixture and beat well.

4. Add the flours gradually and mix until a soft dough forms. Roll out thinly and cut into rounds using a biscuit cutter.

5. Bake until lightly golden.

Easy garlic bread

Garlic bread is always a good idea and this recipe is simple and delicious!

SERVES: 8

450 g sourdough Vienna loaf
  or baguette
125 g butter, softened

5 garlic cloves, crushed
2 tablespoons roughly chopped
  flat-leaf parsley

1. Preheat the oven to 200°C.

2. Cut the bread into 1.5 cm thick slices, being careful not to cut the whole way through.

3. Place the butter, garlic and parsley in a bowl. Mash with a fork until combined. Season with salt and pepper.

4. Spread each cut side of the bread with the butter mixture. Wrap the bread in foil.

5. Place the bread on a baking tray and bake for 15 minutes, or until the butter mixture has melted. Unwrap the garlic bread. Bake for a further 5 minutes, or until golden and crisp.

Toffee apples

Take a walk down memory lane with these old favourites
— toffee apples. The grandkids are sure to love them.

SERVES: 8

8 wooden sticks

8 small red apples, washed and
  dried

1½ cups light corn syrup

300 g unsalted butter, chopped

2 cups caster sugar

2 teaspoons vanilla extract

1. Insert a stick into the centre of each apple and set aside.

2. Place 1 cup of the corn syrup, the butter and sugar in a
    saucepan over medium heat and stir until well combined.
    Bring to the boil and cook for 8–10 minutes (do not stir),
    or until the temperature reaches 140°C (275°F) on a sugar
    thermometer.

3. Remove the corn syrup mixture from the heat and stir in the
    remaining corn syrup and the vanilla.

4. Dip the apples into the caramel and place on a baking tray
    lined with non-stick baking paper. Set aside for 30 minutes,
    or until the toffee is set.

Chicken pasta

'This is my version of chicken carbonara — it's a very quick recipe and healthier than the traditional dish as I use low-fat ingredients.' Elizabeth Wilson

SERVES: 2

2 chicken breasts, diced
3 bacon rashers, sliced
3–4 mushrooms, sliced
1–2 x 185 ml tins low-fat evaporated milk

1 handful low-fat shredded cheese
250 g penne pasta, cooked
1 handful snow peas, sliced spring onions, to taste, chopped

1. Cook the chicken and bacon in a frying pan over medium heat. Add the mushrooms and when cooked, stir in the evaporated milk. Once it begins to boil, sprinkle some shredded cheese in to thicken slightly.

2. Add the cooked pasta and stir through the snow peas and spring onions.

    Note: You can add anything you want to this — it is also tasty with sun-dried tomatoes.

Jam and cream roulade

As yummy as it is pretty, this is the perfect cake for afternoon tea and it will delight all ages.

Serves: 10

oil spray

½ cup plain flour, sifted, plus 2 tablespoons extra, for dusting

3 tablespoons finely ground toasted blanched almonds

pinch of salt

3 large eggs

2 large egg yolks

½ cup granulated sugar

¼ cup unsalted butter, melted

icing sugar, for dusting

1¼ cups strawberry or raspberry jam

1 cup pouring cream

1. Preheat the oven to 200°C. Line a baking tray with baking paper and spray with oil. Lightly dust with flour and tap out the excess. Set aside.

2. In a bowl, combine the ½ cup of flour, the ground almonds and salt and set aside.

3. In a heatproof bowl set over a pan of simmering water, place the eggs, yolks and granulated sugar and whisk until the sugar has dissolved and the mixture is warm to the touch. Using an electric mixer, beat on medium–high speed for 2 minutes. Increase the speed to high and beat for 4 minutes, or until the mixture is pale and thick.

4. Sift the flour mixture over the egg mixture and use a large spatula to carefully fold in. Pour the butter down the side of bowl and gently fold in. Spread the batter onto the prepared tray, making sure it is even. Bake for 7–8 minutes, or until golden brown and springy to the touch.

5. Run a knife around the sides of the cake and turn onto a clean kitchen towel that is dusted with icing sugar. Roll the cake in the towel, starting at a short end. Leave to cool completely, seam side down.

6. Unroll the cake. Spread with the jam, leaving a 1.5 cm border.

7. Whip the cream until soft peaks form. Spread the cream over the jam. Roll the cake without the towel, starting at a short end. Refrigerate for at least 30 minutes and up to 3 hours. Serve dusted with icing sugar.

Gluten-free tomato and bocconcini pizza

This healthy take on pizza makes for a heart-warming meal that is sure to become a family favourite.

SERVES: 4

2 cups gluten-free plain flour

½ cup gluten-free self-raising flour

1 teaspoon salt

1½ teaspoons dry yeast

1 egg, lightly whisked

2 tablespoons olive oil

220 ml warm water

3 ripe tomatoes, roughly chopped

2 garlic cloves, crushed

2 tablespoons tomato paste

1 tablespoon apple cider vinegar

1 teaspoon caster sugar

2 tablespoons small basil leaves, plus extra to serve

16 baby bocconcini, halved

250 g cherry tomatoes

rocket leaves, to serve

1. In a food processor, add the flours, salt and yeast and process until combined. Add the egg, oil and warm water and process again until combined. Turn out onto a clean work surface lightly dusted with gluten-free flour and knead for a few minutes, or until smooth. Place the dough in a lightly oiled bowl and cover with plastic wrap. Set aside in a warm, draught-free spot for 30 minutes, or until it has risen slightly.

2. While the dough is rising, place the chopped tomato, garlic, tomato paste, vinegar and sugar in a saucepan over medium heat and cook, stirring occasionally, for 10 minutes, or until the tomatoes begin to soften and break down. Reduce the heat to low and cook for a further 5 minutes, or until the sauce begins to thicken.

3. Preheat the oven to 200°C. Roll out the dough on a clean work surface dusted with gluten-free flour until you have a smooth base that's large enough to fit a 28 cm round pizza tray.

4. Spread the base with a little of the tomato mixture and sprinkle with the basil leaves. Bake for 15 minutes, or until golden.

5. Spoon the remaining tomato mixture over the base and top with the bocconcini and cherry tomatoes. Bake for 10 minutes, or until the cheese is melted. Top with the rocket and extra basil and serve.

Coconut ice

Teach the grandkids how to make this old favourite. It would have to be one of the prettiest sweet treats we've ever seen. This version is made with condensed milk, which is lower in fat but just as delicious.

MAKES: 64

625 g icing sugar, sifted
3 cups desiccated coconut
395 g tin condensed milk

I egg white
I teaspoon vanilla extract
red food colouring

1. Lightly grease and line the base and sides of a 20 cm square cake tin.

2. In a large bowl, combine the icing sugar and coconut. Add the condensed milk, egg white and vanilla and mix until combined.

3. Divide the mixture between two bowls. Add a few drops of red food colouring to one bowl and mix until combined.

4. Spoon the pink mixture into the prepared tin and press down to even out. Top with the white mixture, pressing down to even out. Cover and refrigerate overnight to set. Cut into 2.5 cm squares to serve.

Beetroot hummus

*For those times when ordinary hummus won't suffice, this beetroot
variety is ready to step in and be the colourful dip you never knew
you needed. It's incredibly simple to make and oh-so delicious.*

MAKES: 2 CUPS

2 beetroots, trimmed, washed
and halved
1½ cups tinned chickpeas,
drained and rinsed
3 tablespoons tahini paste
2 garlic cloves, peeled

3 tablespoons lemon juice
2 tablespoons vegetable stock
coriander leaves, chopped, to
serve
olive oil, to serve

1. To cook the beetroot, place in the microwave on high for
    10–15 minutes, or until tender. When they've cooled a little,
    slide the beetroot out of their skins and chop roughly.

2. Place all the ingredients in a blender or food processor and
    process until smooth.

3. Serve with the coriander sprinkled on top and drizzle with
    the olive oil.

Caramel slice

With layers of chocolate, biscuits and gooey caramel, each bite of these delectable caramel slices will be a moment of food heaven.

MAKES: 16

1 cup plain flour
½ cup soft brown sugar
½ cup desiccated coconut
125 g unsalted butter, melted,
  plus 100 g extra

2 x 395 g tins sweetened
  condensed milk
⅓ cup golden syrup
200 g dark chocolate, melted
1 tablespoon vegetable oil

1. Preheat the oven to 180°C. Lightly grease an 18 cm x
    28 cm slice tin and line with baking paper.

2. Combine the flour, sugar and coconut in a bowl. Add the
    melted butter and mix well. Press the mixture firmly into
    the prepared tin. Bake for 15–20 minutes, or until lightly
    browned. Leave to cool.

3. Place the extra butter, condensed milk and golden syrup in
    a saucepan. Stir over low heat until smooth. Pour over the
    base. Bake for 20–25 minutes, or until golden. Leave to
    cool.

4. Combine the dark chocolate and oil, stir until smooth, then
    pour evenly over the slice. Cut into squares to serve.

Note: To save money on ingredients, opt for no-name
brands.

Lemon and chicken parmesan rissoles

This recipe puts a delicious spin on an old-time favourite that is guaranteed to delight little ones.

SERVES: 4

500 g chicken mince
1 egg, lightly beaten
2 garlic cloves, crushed
½ cup fresh breadcrumbs
1 tablespoon finely chopped
    basil leaves
1 teaspoon finely grated lemon
    zest

¼ cup pitted kalamata olives,
    chopped
⅓ cup finely grated parmesan
    cheese
¼ cup plain flour
1 tablespoon olive oil

1. Preheat the oven to 180°C.

2. Combine the mince, egg, garlic, breadcrumbs, basil, lemon
    zest, olives and parmesan in a bowl.

3. Place the flour on a plate. Using the mixture, shape into
    eight 2 cm thick rissoles. Roll in the flour to lightly coat.
    Place on a large plate. Cover and refrigerate for 20 minutes.

4. Heat the oil in a frying pan over medium heat. Cook the
    rissoles, in batches, for 1–2 minutes, or until browned.
    Transfer to a greased baking tray. Bake for 8–10 minutes, or
    until cooked through.

Fresh strawberry jelly

A simple, fruity dessert that's great for adults and kids alike!

SERVES: 6

2 x 250 g punnets strawberries, hulled and chopped
½ cup water
¼ cup caster sugar

1½ tablespoons powdered gelatine
2 cups clear apple or orange juice
whipped cream, to decorate

1. Blend half the strawberries in a food processor or blender until smooth. Strain the mixture through a sieve to remove the seeds. Discard the pulp.

2. Combine the water and caster sugar in a saucepan over medium heat. Add the gelatine and stir until the sugar and gelatine are dissolved.

3. Add the juice and strawberry purée. Mixing thoroughly for 5 minutes, or until the liquid just comes to a simmer. Set aside to cool.

4. Meanwhile, place the remaining strawberries in the base of six glasses. Pour the jelly mixture over the strawberries. Refrigerate for at least 4 hours, or until set. Serve with the whipped cream and decorate with strawberry leaves, if desired.

Banana split toasted sandwich

Perfect for breakfast, lunch or treat time, this old-school favourite can also be made to take out and about for a meal-on-the-run.

SERVES: 1

30 g butter
2 slices bread

50 g chocolate hazelnut spread
½ banana, sliced

1. Preheat the sandwich press or jaffle to medium–high heat. Butter one side of the two slices of bread.

2. Spread the chocolate hazelnut spread on both of the non-buttered sides of the bread. Layer the banana slices on the hazelnut spread side of one of the slices of bread. Place the other slice on top, with the buttered side facing up.

3. Grill the sandwich for 3 minutes, or until toasted. Cut the sandwich in half and serve immediately.

Chocolate chip cookies

*A classic recipe for one of life's little pleasures ... the humble —
but very satisfying — chocolate chip cookie. Be warned, with a
soft squidgy middle these may cause excessive indulgence.*

MAKES: 14

150 g butter, softened
80 g soft brown sugar
80 g caster sugar
2 teaspoons vanilla extract
1 large egg

225 g plain flour
½ teaspoon bicarbonate of soda
¼ teaspoon salt
200 g plain chocolate chips or
chunks

1. Preheat the oven to 190°C. Line two baking trays with non-stick baking paper.

2. Using an electric mixer, beat the butter and sugars in a bowl until creamy. Beat in the vanilla and egg. Sift the flour, bicarbonate of soda and salt and add to the mixture. Mix well to combine. Add the chocolate chips and stir well.

3. Using a teaspoon, place small mounds of the mixture, spaced well apart, on the baking trays. Bake in the oven for 8–10 minutes, or until light brown on the edges and still slightly soft in the centre.

4. Leave on the tray for a couple of minutes to firm up, then transfer to a wire rack to cool completely.

Strawberry yoghurt pops

For a healthy and delicious treat, try these super-simple yoghurt pops. Little ones will have loads of fun making them.

MAKES: 8

2 punnets strawberries, hulled and chopped

1 cup vanilla yoghurt

1. Process the strawberries in a food processor until smooth. Transfer to a bowl.

2. Add the vanilla yoghurt and gently fold until the mixture is just combined.

3. Spoon the strawberry mixture evenly among eight 80 ml (⅓ cup) capacity ice-block moulds. Place in the freezer for 8 hours, or until firm.

   Note: You can replace strawberries with any other fruit — mangos work really well too!

Easy lunches

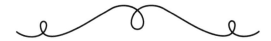

'*The thing I absolutely love about food is it's a common thread that connects us no matter what culture we come from.*'
— *Poh Ling Yeow*

Whether you're having a quick lunch at home, preparing something for loved ones or want to pack something to take on the run, your midday meal can venture further than a regular old sandwich and still be easy to prepare. From soups to quick pasta dishes, these pages are full of inspiring options that are easy to whip up.

Nettle soup

'At the end of World War II, food in the UK was in short supply. My father, who had returned from the Far East, decided to use nettles and also dandelions as salad veggies, and cooked the nettles as you would cabbage.' Bill Humble

SERVES: 4

10 large handfuls nettle leaves
2 teaspoons celery salt
1 teaspoon black pepper
1 teaspoon curry powder
1 teaspoon turmeric
1 large onion, chopped
8 garlic cloves

dash of worcestershire sauce
½ cup soy sauce
pinch of sugar
1 teaspoon ground ginger
1 teaspoon onion powder
1 teaspoon unsalted butter or
   sour cream, to serve

1. Combine all of the ingredients in a saucepan and bring to a simmer for 20 minutes. Set aside to cool.

2. Using a food processor, blend to the desired consistency.

3. Serve warm with a knob of unsalted butter or sour cream.

   Note: I sometimes add cooked potato, carrot, turnip, parsnip, celery, fresh herbs of choice, and a bit of this and a bit of that, all blended. A creamy, health-packed soup to give you longevity.

Last-minute carbonara

'I have been using this recipe for 20 years. My kids loved it and it's a great standby when the cupboard is bare.' Kathryn Ebert

SERVES: 4

4–5 bacon rashers, cut into
  thick strips
300 ml pouring cream
1 egg, lightly beaten
150 g shredded tasty cheese

1 tablespoon grated parmesan
  cheese
1 teaspoon chopped parsley
  (optional)
pinch of pepper
500 g fettuccine

1. Cook the bacon in a deep frying pan over medium heat until crispy.

2. Using an electric mixer, beat the cream and egg together.

3. Add the cheeses, parsley (if using) and pepper to the cream mixture and stir well to combine.

4. Pour the sauce into the frying pan with the bacon and cook for 4–6 minutes.

5. Meanwhile, cook the pasta in a large saucepan of boiling salted water, following packet directions, until al dente. Drain well. Return to the saucepan.

6. Add the sauce to the cooked pasta and gently toss over low heat for 1–2 minutes, or until heated through. Serve immediately.

Variation: You can also add mushrooms to the sauce mixture.

Ploughman's toastie

SERVES: 1

2 slices fresh white bread

30 g butter

1 tablespoon pickles

2 thick slices ham

2 thick slices cheddar cheese

¼ red apple, grated

2–3 lettuce leaves

1. Preheat the sandwich press or jaffle to medium–high heat. Butter both sides of the 2 slices of bread.

2. Layer all the ingredients between the slices of bread.

3. Grill the sandwich for 3 minutes, or until toasted. Cut the sandwich in half and serve immediately.

Brown rice, lentil and feta salad

'My aunty used to make this and even as a child I loved it. I think as time went on she modified it as I don't think you could buy rocket in those days.' Sue Fraser

SERVES: 6

3 cups cooked brown rice, cooled

2 cups brown lentils, drained and rinsed

1 red capsicum, roasted, diced

1 cup sultanas

1 cup rocket, chopped

2 spring onions, chopped

½ cup chopped parsley

½ cup chopped mint

½ cup chopped coriander

100 g feta cheese

½ cup lemon juice

3 tablespoons olive oil

toasted slivered almonds and pine nuts, to garnish

1. Combine the rice, lentils, capsicum and sultanas in a large bowl.

2. Add the rocket, spring onions and chopped herbs and toss well to combine.

3. Crumble the feta cheese over the top and drizzle with the lemon juice and oil. Stand the salad for 1 hour to allow the flavours to develop.

4. Sprinkle the salad with the almonds and pine nuts and serve.

Fifteen-minute spaghetti with rocket pesto

*Served hot in winter or cold on a summer's evening,
this pesto pasta packs a flavoursome punch. And what's
more — you will have dinner ready in 15 minutes.*

SERVES: 4

400 g spaghetti
grated parmesan cheese, to
  serve
baby rocket leaves, to serve
Rocket pesto
1 bunch rocket, trimmed
½ cup basil leaves

⅓ cup grated parmesan cheese
⅓ cup toasted walnuts
2 tablespoons toasted pine nuts
1 garlic clove
½ cup extra virgin olive oil
salt and pepper, to season

1. To make the rocket pesto, place the rocket, basil, parmesan, walnuts, pine nuts and garlic in a food processor and process until finely chopped. While the motor is running, gradually add the oil in a thin, steady stream until incorporated. Taste and season with salt and pepper.

2. Cook the pasta in a large saucepan of boiling salted water, following packet directions, until al dente. Drain well and return to the pan with the pesto. Gently toss to combine.

3. Serve immediately, with the parmesan cheese and rocket.

The Way Mum Made It

Quick and easy spicy pumpkin soup

Ruth Weston

SERVES: 6

1 tablespoon coconut oil
1 onion, chopped
1–2 tablespoons Thai red curry
    paste
1 kg Japanese or blue pumpkin,
    roughly diced

3 large potatoes, roughly diced
2 vegetable stock cubes,
    crumbled
½ x 270 ml tin coconut cream
garlic bread or crusty bread, to
    serve (optional)

1. Melt the coconut oil in a saucepan over medium heat. Add the onion and curry paste and cook, stirring, until the onion is translucent.

2. Add the pumpkin and potato, crumbled stock cubes and enough water to almost cover. Simmer until the pumpkin and potato are cooked.

3. Remove from the heat and purée, using a stick blender or food processor, until smooth.

4. Add the coconut cream and mix well. Serve warm, with garlic bread, if desired.

   Note: When selecting pumpkin, choose the deepest orange colour as they are the sweetest and have more flavour.

Simple tabouli

*This delicious salad makes the most of fresh ingredients
and works well with any grilled meat.*

SERVES: 4

1 teaspoon lemon zest
3 tablespoons lemon juice
3 tablespoons olive oil
salt and pepper, to season
¼ cup cracked burghul

1 bunch flat-leaf parsley, finely
  chopped
2 cucumbers, diced
2 tomatoes, diced
½ small red onion, finely diced

1. Place the lemon zest, lemon juice, olive oil and salt and
   pepper in a bowl with the burghul and allow to soak for
   30 minutes.

2. Place the parsley, cucumber, tomato and onion in a large
   bowl. Add the burghul mixture. Toss to combine and serve
   immediately, or refrigerate to allow the flavours to develop
   further.

Mock chicken dip

'This recipe is handwritten by Mum in my own recipe book. I have been making it all my married life and find it very handy for "Happy Hours" on the road. It has been shared with many Grey Nomads over our many years of travelling this great land. My mum, who is now 92, often made this delicious dip when guests were coming over at short notice. Everyone has the ingredients in their pantry and it's so easy to make. Tastes good on crackers or sandwiches and the ingredients can be doubled or tripled.' Sue Ferguson

MAKES: 1 CUP

1 tablespoon butter

1 tablespoon diced onion

1 tomato, peeled and diced

1 teaspoon dried mixed herbs

salt and pepper, to season

1 tablespoon tasty cheese, grated

1 egg, lightly beaten

1. Heat the butter in a saucepan over medium heat until just melted. Add the onion, tomato and mixed herbs. Season to taste. Simmer gently until the ingredients are soft.

2. Add the cheese and egg. As soon as the egg is cooked, remove from the heat. Allow to cool, then refrigerate until needed.

    Note: This dip will keep in the refrigerator for up to 7 days.

Cobb salad

SERVES: 2

1 chicken breast
2 rashers bacon, cut into strips
1 baby cos lettuce, roughly torn
1 avocado, thinly sliced
200 g cherry tomatoes,
    quartered

2 hard-boiled eggs, peeled and
    sliced
½ red onion, diced
2 tablespoons crumbled feta
    cheese
your choice of dressing

1. Slice the chicken breast in half to make two thinner pieces.
    Cook the chicken in a frying pan over medium heat until
    cooked through. Set aside for a few minutes, then cut into
    strips.

2. Cook the bacon in the frying pan over medium heat until
    crispy.

3. Place the lettuce in a large bowl and then arrange the rest of
    your ingredients on top in clumps, crumbling the feta over
    the top and drizzling with your favourite dressing. Serve
    immediately.

Chicken and rice soup

'As a student teacher at Christ College, Oakleigh, I used to buy this delicious chicken and rice soup. I worked at replicating it and after 42 years, I have done a reasonably good job.' Sharon Buxton

MAKES: 6 BOWLS

1 chicken breast
salt and pepper, to season
1 large carrot, finely diced
1 large onion, finely diced

1 large handful parsley, finely chopped
1 cup rice
2 chicken stock cubes, crumbled

1. Place the chicken breast in a pot, cover with cold water and add salt and pepper. Bring to the boil over medium heat, then simmer until tender. Set aside to cool.

2. When cooled, remove the chicken from the pot (keep the broth) and dice. Return the diced chicken to the pot with the kept chicken broth.

3. Add the carrot, onion and parsley to the pot. Stir to combine, then add the rice and crumbled chicken stock cubes. Add more water, stirring. Bring to the boil, then simmer until the rice and vegetables are cooked. Add more water if needed. Season to taste.

Note: Don't worry if initially the soup looks too thick as you can add water and seasoning to your required taste.

Noodle omelette

'My mum showed me this recipe for a quick snack for lunch or dinner. It is so easy.' Margaret Larkins

SERVES: 2–3

1 x 72 g packet instant noodles
50 g ham or bacon, finely chopped
1 tomato, finely chopped

2 spring onions or 1 onion, finely sliced
1 tablespoon oil or butter
4 eggs
salt and pepper, to season

1. Cook the noodles according to the packet directions, adding the flavour sachet if desired. Drain well.

2. Add the noodles, ham or bacon, tomato and onion to a bowl and toss to combine.

3. Heat the oil or butter in a frying pan over medium heat. Add the noodle mixture and cook for 1–2 minutes, or until heated through.

4. Pour the egg mixture over the noodles and cook for a further 2–3 minutes, or until the egg is set. Season to taste. Cut into wedges and serve.

The Way Mum Made It

Tuna and olive pasta

For a light and refreshing meal, this tried-and-tested combination of tuna and olives is for you.

SERVES: 4

500 g penne pasta
1 tablespoon olive oil
2 garlic cloves, crushed
¼ teaspoon dried chilli flakes
salt and pepper, to season

500 g cherry tomatoes, halved
1 x 425 g tin tuna in olive oil, drained
125 g pitted black olives

1. Cook the pasta in a large saucepan of boiling salted water, following packet directions, until al dente.

2. Meanwhile, heat the oil in a frying pan over medium heat. Fry the garlic and chilli flakes until softened. Season with salt and pepper. Add the tomatoes, and cover and cook for 3 minutes, or until softened.

3. Stir in the tuna and olives. Using a fork, flake the tuna. Cook for a further 2 minutes, or until heated through.

4. Toss the tuna mixture through the pasta and serve immediately.

Swagman's roll

'When I started making this 25 years ago it was an instant hit with the family and continues to delight my children and grandchildren. I love it because it is easier than making pies.' Diane Riordon

SERVES: 4–6

1 tablespoon oil
500 g beef mince
1 onion, diced
1 teaspoon beef stock powder

½ cup tomato sauce
4 sheets puff pastry
1 tablespoon milk

1. Preheat the oven to 180°C. Line a baking tray with baking paper.

2. Heat the oil in a frying pan over medium heat. Add the mince and cook, stirring, until browned.

3. Add the onion, stock powder and tomato sauce. Simmer until cooked and the liquid evaporates. Set aside to cool.

4. Roll out the pastry to form a rectangle. Spread the mince over the pastry, leaving a 1 cm border around the edge. Moisten the edges with the milk and roll up from the long side like a Swiss roll.

5. Place on the prepared tray. Cut slits along the top and brush the top with the remaining milk. Bake for 15–20 minutes, or until golden brown. Serve warm, cut in slices on an angle.

Tangy coleslaw

SERVES: 4

1 x 400 g bag fine-cut coleslaw
2 tablespoons toasted pine nuts
Dressing
2 tablespoons sweet chilli sauce
2 tablespoons lemon juice

1 tablespoon tamari or soy
  sauce
1 teaspoon soy sauce
1 teaspoon olive oil

1. Combine all of the dressing ingredients in a jug and whisk.

2. Rinse the coleslaw ingredients and drain well. Add to a large serving bowl with the pine nuts.

3. Pour over the dressing and toss gently to combine.

Classic club sandwich

SERVES: 4

12 slices bread
12 shortcut bacon rashers
olive oil spray
½ cup whole-egg mayonnaise

12 lettuce leaves
320 g sliced turkey breast
4 ripe tomatoes, sliced
salt and pepper, to season

1. Preheat an oven grill to medium. Place half the bread under the grill and toast for 1–2 minutes on each side, or until lightly toasted. Repeat with the remaining bread.

2. Lightly spray both sides of the bacon with oil. Place under the grill and cook for 2–3 minutes on each side, or until crispy. Place on paper towels to absorb excess oil.

3. Spread 8 of the slices of toast with the mayonnaise. Arrange half of the lettuce, turkey and tomato over 4 slices. Season with salt and pepper.

4. Top with a second slice of toast with mayonnaise. Then add the remaining lettuce, bacon and tomato. Season well with salt and pepper. Top with the remaining pieces of toast. Use toothpicks to secure.

Fresh pea, mint and bacon salad

This crisp pea and mint salad is the perfect combination of fresh, summer flavours with a sprinkling of indulgence via the bacon and cheese.

SERVES: 4

3 bacon rashers
1 cup shelled green peas
270 g rocket leaves
¼ cup chopped mint
1½ tablespoons lemon juice

1 tablespoon extra virgin olive oil
salt and pepper, to season
½ cup shaved pecorino cheese

1. Cook the bacon in a frying pan over medium heat until crispy. Allow to cool slightly, then roughly chop into small pieces.

2. Bring 2 cups of water to the boil in a saucepan over medium heat. Add the peas and cook for 1 minute. Drain and plunge the peas into iced water, then drain again.

3. Combine the peas, rocket and mint in a large bowl. Add the lemon juice, olive oil and bacon, and season with salt and pepper. Toss well. Sprinkle with the pecorino cheese. Serve immediately.

Chicken pie

Looking for something impressive (but quite easy) to make? Look no further than this scrumptious pie. Served with a salad, it's a delicious meal for summer that will impress the entire family.

SERVES: 4–6

4 tablespoons butter
¼ cup chopped onion
¼ cup chopped celery
¼ cup chopped carrot
¼ teaspoon salt
2 tablespoons plain flour
2 cups milk
½ cup thick cream
1 cube chicken stock, dissolved
    in hot water

2 cups cooked chopped chicken
½ cup frozen peas
½ teaspoon thyme, plus extra
    for garnishing
1 large sheet frozen shortcrust
    pastry, thawed
1 sheet puff pastry
1 egg, beaten

1. Melt the butter in a large saucepan over medium–high heat. Add the onion, celery, carrot and salt and sauté until the onion is translucent and the vegetables start to get tender. Sprinkle the flour over the vegetables and cook for 1–2 minutes.

2. Gradually whisk in the milk, cream and chicken stock and bring to a slow boil. Simmer gently over medium heat for 5 minutes, or until the sauce begins to thicken.

3. Reduce the heat to low and add the chicken, peas and thyme. Preheat the oven to 220°C.

4. Line the base and side of a pie dish with the shortcrust pastry. Trim the edge. Line with baking paper and fill with rice or dried beans. Blind bake for 10 minutes. Remove the paper and rice or dried beans and bake for a further 8 minutes, or until the pastry is lightly golden. Remove from the oven and leave to cool slightly.

5. Pour the chicken mixture into the pie dish. Place the sheet of puff pastry over the top to enclose the filling. Use a sharp knife to trim the edge.

6. Using a pastry brush, brush the puff pastry with the egg. Bake for 30–35 minutes, or until the puff pastry is a deep golden brown colour. Leave to cool for 5 minutes before serving.

Three-bean salad

SERVES: 4–8

400 g tin cannellini beans,
rinsed and drained

400 g tin kidney beans, rinsed
and drained

400 g tin chickpeas, rinsed and
drained

400 g tin corn kernels, drained

2 celery stalks, finely chopped

½ red capsicum, chopped

½ red onion, finely chopped

mint leaves, to garnish

Dressing

¼ cup red wine vinegar

1 tablespoon extra-virgin olive
oil

1 garlic clove, crushed

pinch of dried oregano

salt and pepper, to season

1. In a large bowl, combine the cannellini beans, kidney
   beans, chickpeas, corn, celery, capsicum and onion.

2. In a separate small bowl, whisk together the dressing
   ingredients.

3. Drizzle the dressing over the salad and toss to coat.
   Refrigerate for a few hours to allow the flavours to develop.
   Garnish with the mint and serve.

The Way Mum Made It

Risoni salad

Rosie Kennett

SERVES: 4–6

350 g risoni
¼ cup olive oil
I cup pine nuts
½ cup currants
2 garlic cloves, crushed
juice of I lemon
I teaspoon ground cumin
I teaspoon turmeric

½ teaspoon sugar
I small green capsicum
2 tablespoons chopped
  coriander
2 tablespoons chopped mint
2 tablespoons chopped parsley
salt and pepper, to season

1. Cook the risoni in a large saucepan of boiling salted water, following packet directions, until al dente. Drain well and set aside.

2. Heat I tablespoon of the olive oil in a small frying pan over medium heat. Add the pine nuts and currants and cook for 1–2 minutes. Remove the pan from the heat.

3. Add the garlic, lemon juice, cumin, turmeric, sugar and the remaining oil. Stir well to combine and set aside to cool completely.

4. In a large serving bowl, combine the risoni, capsicum, coriander, mint and parsley. Add the pine nut mixture and toss gently to combine. Season to taste and serve immediately.

Pumpkin and chickpea salad

This salad is tasty enough to enjoy as a main meal
or as a great side dish to roasted meals.

SERVES: 4

½ butternut pumpkin, skin
   and seeds removed, cut into
   2 cm pieces
1 teaspoon ground cumin
1 teaspoon sweet paprika
salt and pepper, to season

1 x 400 g tin chickpeas,
   drained and rinsed
60 g English spinach
2 tablespoons olive oil
1 tablespoon red wine vinegar

1. Preheat the oven to 200°C. Lightly grease a large roasting
    tin with olive oil.

2. Arrange the pumpkin pieces in the tin and sprinkle with the
    cumin and paprika. Season with salt and pepper. Toss the
    pumpkin pieces until they are well coated.

3. Roast for 20–25 minutes, or until golden and tender,
    turning the pumpkin pieces once.

4. Add the chickpeas to the tin and roast for a further
    5–8 minutes. Remove from the heat. Add the spinach and
    toss together.

5. Whisk the olive oil and vinegar together. Drizzle over the
    pumpkin and chickpeas. Serve warm.

Cheesy pea and pesto pasta

*Not only will this pasta dish tick some of your daily
nutritional boxes, it's simple to make, vegetarian and you
can add or subtract ingredients according to taste.*

SERVES: 2

140 g pasta of your choice
1 tablespoon olive oil
½ onion, finely chopped
1 garlic clove, finely chopped or
   grated
85 g frozen peas, thawed

110 g tasty cheese, grated
1 tablespoon pesto
100 ml thick cream
salt and pepper, to season
1 handful parsley, chopped

1. Cook the pasta in a large saucepan of boiling salted water,
    following packet directions, until al dente. Drain well and
    set aside.

2. Heat the oil in a large frying pan over medium heat. Gently
    fry the onion and garlic for a few minutes, to soften. Stir in
    the peas and cook for a few minutes, until heated through.

3. Stir in the cheese and pesto, then add the cream. Season
    with salt and pepper. Cook for a further 4–5 minutes,
    stirring. Add the parsley (leaving 1 tablespoon to garnish)
    and the cooked pasta. Stir gently to combine.

4. Transfer to a serving bowl or plate and serve immediately,
    garnished with the remaining parsley.

Niçoise salad

SERVES: 4

12 small new potatoes, halved
400 g baby green beans,
  trimmed
1 x 425 g tin tuna in oil,
  drained, flaked
250 g grape tomatoes, halved
¾ cup black olives
2 baby cos lettuces, leaves
  separated

4 hard-boiled eggs, peeled,
  quartered
Dressing
4 tablespoons olive oil
4 tablespoons red wine vinegar
1 tablespoon dijon mustard
salt and pepper

1. To make the dressing, whisk the oil, vinegar and mustard in a jug. Season with salt and pepper.

2. Cook the potatoes in a large saucepan of boiling water for 10 minutes, or until just tender. Transfer to a large bowl.

3. Add the green beans to the pan. Cook for 2–3 minutes, or until bright green and just tender. Drain. Refresh under cold water. Drain again. Add the beans to the potato.

4. Add the tuna, tomatoes, olives, lettuce and egg to the potato mixture. Add the prepared dressing. Toss gently to combine. Season with salt and pepper.

The Way Mum Made It

Delicious dinners

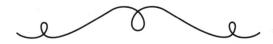

*'Dining with one's friends and beloved family is
certainly one of life's primal and most innocent delights,
one that is both soul-satisfying and eternal.'*
— Julia Child

Dinner, whether eaten alone or shared with loved ones,
is one of the loveliest times of day. It's an opportunity
to sit down, unwind, shake off the day and feed the
body and soul. Not only is it a chance to relax but if
you are gathering around with family and friends, it's
a good time to come together and spend quality time
catching up. What better way to do this than over a
delicious meal? Dip into our chapter brimming with
yummy options. Be warned: you'll want to cook them
all at once.

Lemon and rosemary chicken

'A low-fat recipe used for years that is especially good if you're trying to lose weight.' Julia O'Keeffe

SERVES: 2

6 chicken tenderloins (or
  2 chicken breast pieces,
  each cut into 3 long pieces,
  flattened)
plain flour, for dusting
pepper, to season

2 tablespoons oil
1 teaspoon dried rosemary
zest and juice of 2 lemons
chopped chives or parsley, to
  garnish

1. Flatten the chicken between plastic wrap. Coat both sides with the flour and pepper and shake off the excess.

2. Heat the oil in a frying pan over medium heat. Add the chicken and rosemary and cook until the chicken is cooked through.

3. Sprinkle over some of the lemon zest. Add the lemon juice. Garnish with the chopped chives or parsley and the remaining lemon zest.

Tuna mornay bake

*Healthy and delicious, get your dose of omega-3 fatty acids
with this no-fuss tuna mornay that is quick to make.*

SERVES: 4

200 g elbow macaroni

1 tablespoon olive oil

1 onion, chopped

2 teaspoons crushed garlic
cloves

1 x 425 g tin tuna chunks in
springwater, drained

½ cup semi-dried tomatoes,
chopped

½ cup pitted kalamata olives,
halved

300 ml pouring cream

¼ cup shredded parmesan
cheese

2 tablespoons flat-leaf parsley,
chopped, to serve

1. Cook the pasta in a large saucepan of boiling salted water,
    following packet directions, until al dente. Drain well.

2. Meanwhile, heat the oil in a frying pan over medium–high
    heat. Add the onion and cook for 1–2 minutes, or until
    softened. Add the garlic. Cook for 30 seconds. Add the
    tuna, tomatoes, olives, cream and the cooked pasta. Stir for
    2–3 minutes, or until heated through.

3. Preheat the grill on high. Put the pasta mixture into an
    ovenproof dish and sprinkle with the parmesan. Cook
    under the grill for 4–5 minutes, or until golden and bubbly.
    Sprinkle with the parsley and serve.

Lamb shank dinner

'Fifty years ago I found a little snippet in the local paper with this recipe on it. I thought I would try it … it has been a family favourite ever since. I have lost track of how many copies I have handed on.' Daphne Baldock

SERVES: 4

1 tablespoon butter, plus
  1 tablespoon for the roux
1 tablespoon oil
4 lamb shanks
1 large onion, finely chopped
2 teaspoons worcestershire
  sauce

2 cups chicken stock
2 potatoes, quartered
3 carrots, cut into chunks
2 cups green peas
1 tablespoon fruit chutney
1 tablespoon plain flour
2 tablespoons parsley, chopped

1. Heat the butter and oil in a heavy-based saucepan over medium heat. Add the lamb shanks and slowly brown on all sides.

2. Add the onion, worcestershire sauce and stock and bring to the boil. Cover and simmer for 1 hour.

3. Add the vegetables, cover and simmer until the meat is almost falling off the bone and the vegetables are cooked through. Stir through the chutney.

4. At this stage I make a roux – 1 tablespoon of butter and 1 tablespoon of plain flour. You may need to add a bit more flour – the paste needs to be slightly stiff. Gently stir the roux through the casserole to thicken the sauce.

5. Season to taste and serve with the chopped parsley.

   Note: The roux was not in the original recipe but we like the sauce slightly thicker.

Chicken, bacon and pumpkin pasta bake

*Once autumn gets underway it is time to start planning dinners for a
cosy night in. Hearty and warming, this pasta bake is just the ticket.*

SERVES: 6

500 g butternut pumpkin,
   cut into I cm cubes
1½ tablespoons olive oil
salt and pepper, to season
500 g macaroni
400 g chicken breast fillets
2 bacon rashers, trimmed

60 g butter
⅓ cup plain flour
3 cups milk
1½ cups grated tasty cheese
50 g baby spinach
½ cup grated parmesan cheese

1. Preheat the oven to 180°C. Line a large baking tray with
    baking paper.

2. Place the pumpkin on the prepared tray. Drizzle with
    1 tablespoon of oil. Season with salt and pepper. Toss to
    coat. Roast for 20–25 minutes, or until golden and tender.
    Set aside.

3. Meanwhile, cook the pasta in a large saucepan of boiling
    salted water, following packet directions, until al dente.
    Drain well. Place in a large bowl.

4. Heat the remaining oil in a large non-stick frying pan over medium–high heat. Add the chicken and reduce the heat to medium. Cook for 4–5 minutes on each side, or until cooked through. Transfer to a plate.

5. Add the bacon to the pan. Cook for 2–3 minutes on each side, or until golden. Roughly chop the bacon and chicken. Add to the pasta.

6. Melt the butter in a saucepan over medium heat until foaming. Add the flour. Cook, stirring with a wooden spoon, for 1–2 minutes, or until the mixture bubbles. Remove from the heat. Stir in the milk until smooth. Return to the heat. Cook, stirring, for 4–5 minutes, or until the mixture boils and thickens. Stir in the tasty cheese. Season with salt and pepper.

7. Lightly grease a 3 litre ovenproof dish. Add the pumpkin, spinach and sauce to the pasta mixture. Stir to combine. Spoon into the prepared dish. Sprinkle with the parmesan. Bake for 20 minutes at 180°C, or until golden.

Veal casserole

*'My aunt Grace introduced the family to this rich recipe and it
has been a great favourite in the family.' Meg Snodgrass*

SERVES: 6

500 g assorted vegetables, such
 as pumpkin, zucchini, carrot
 and onion, cut into 2 cm
 pieces
1 cup dry breadcrumbs
½ cup tomato sauce

3 tablespoons worcestershire
 sauce
1 kg veal steaks
5 bacon rashers, chopped
150 ml red wine
salt and pepper, to season

1. Preheat the oven to 150°C. Place a layer of vegetables
 in a large casserole dish. Sprinkle one-quarter of the
 breadcrumbs over, then dot with one-quarter of the tomato
 and worcestershire sauces.

2. Add a layer of veal and some of the bacon. Cover with
 another quarter of the breadcrumbs and dot with a little of
 the remaining tomato and worcestershire sauces.

3. Repeat the layers, finishing with the bacon under the
 breadcrumbs. Pour the wine over the layers, being careful
 not to wash off the breadcrumbs, and season with salt and
 pepper.

4. Cook, covered, for 3 hours. Serve with mashed or oven-
 baked potatoes.

Note 1: This can be cooked without the wine, substituting water or stock.

Note 2: If too moist, remove the lid for the last 30 minutes of cooking.

Note 3: You can use cheaper cuts of steak for this recipe if you like — it'll still be delicious!

Minestrone soup

SERVES: 4

2½ tablespoons olive oil

3 bacon rashers, rind removed, roughly chopped

2 carrots, chopped

2 celery stalks, chopped

1 potato, chopped

2 garlic cloves, crushed

1 litre beef stock

1 x 400 g tin red kidney beans, rinsed and drained

1 x 400 g tin diced tomatoes

1 cup pasta

salt and pepper, to season

1. Heat the oil in a large saucepan over high heat. Add the bacon, carrot, celery, potato and garlic and stir to combine. Cook, uncovered and stirring often, for 5 minutes.

2. Add the stock, red kidney beans and tomatoes to the pan, cover and bring to the boil. Reduce the heat to medium–low. Simmer, covered, stirring occasionally, for 30 minutes, or until the vegetables are tender.

3. Increase the heat to high. Add the pasta and cook, following packet directions, until the pasta is al dente. Season with salt and pepper. Ladle into serving bowls and serve immediately.

Note: This will keep in the freezer for 4–6 months.

Cranberry chicken

'I got this recipe years ago from a friend and now it's been passed on to many others. It's so simple but has a sensational taste and is worth trying.' Helen Woodward

SERVES: 4

4 chicken breast fillets
½ x 40 g packet French onion
  soup mix

½ cup orange juice
½ cup cranberry sauce

1. Preheat the oven to 180°C. Place the chicken in an ovenproof dish.

2. Combine the soup mix, orange juice and cranberry sauce in a bowl. Pour the mixture over the chicken and leave to marinate for 1 hour.

3. Bake for 40 minutes. Serve warm with a green salad.

Quiche Lorraine

*You can't go past the simple yet very tasty quiche Lorraine.
It's quick to pop in the oven and tastes delicious.*

SERVES: 8

2 sheets ready-rolled shortcrust
pastry
1 tablespoon olive oil
1 onion, finely chopped
4 bacon rashers, rind removed,
finely chopped

1 cup grated tasty cheese
3 eggs
1 teaspoon plain flour
300 ml pouring cream
½ cup milk
salt and pepper, to season

1. Preheat the oven to 200°C. Lightly grease a 23 cm loose-based flan tin.

2. Line the base and sides of the tin with the pastry and trim the excess. Line the pastry with baking paper. Half-fill with dried beans or rice. Bake for 10 minutes, then remove the paper and beans. Bake for a further 10 minutes, or until golden. Reduce the oven temperature to 180°C.

3. Heat the oil in a frying pan over medium–high heat. Add the onion and bacon and cook for 3 minutes. Drain on paper towels and leave to cool.

4. Sprinkle the bacon mixture over the pastry and top with the cheese.

5. Whisk the remaining ingredients in a jug. Pour over the bacon mixture.

6. Place the tin on a baking tray. Bake for 30–35 minutes, or until set. Stand for 5 minutes before serving.

Tomato and beef macaroni

'This recipe was given to me by my mother-in-law many years ago.' Dianne Gemmell

SERVES: 4–6

1 tablespoon butter or oil
2 bacon rashers, chopped
½ cup chopped green capsicum
1 celery stalk, chopped
1 large onion, chopped
2 garlic cloves, minced
500 g lean beef mince

1 tablespoon curry powder
2 tablespoons tomato paste
1 cup chicken stock
salt and pepper, to season
2 cups cooked macaroni
1 cup grated tasty cheese

1. Preheat the oven to 180°C. Lightly grease a casserole dish.

2. Heat the butter in a large non-stick frying pan over medium heat. Cook the bacon, capsicum, celery, onion and garlic for 2–3 minutes.

3. Add the mince and cook until browned. Stir in the curry powder and continue cooking for 2 minutes. Add the tomato paste and stock and mix through. Season with salt and pepper and stir through the cooked macaroni.

4. Spoon the mixture into the casserole dish and sprinkle with the grated cheese. Bake for approximately 30 minutes. Serve warm with your choice of vegetables or salad.

The Way Mum Made It

Cauliflower cheese

*This classic side dish is sure to impress and might even
steal the thunder to become a favourite main.*

SERVES: 6

1 large cauliflower, cut into
    florets
50 g butter
5 tablespoons plain flour
1 cup milk
1 tablespoon dijon mustard

¼ cup fine dry breadcrumbs
1 cup grated strong cheddar
    cheese
salt and pepper, to season
dill, to garnish (optional)

1. Preheat the oven to 200°C.

2. Bring a saucepan of salted water to the boil and add the
    cauliflower. Cook for 10 minutes, or until tender. Drain
    and set aside.

3. Melt the butter in a saucepan over low heat. Stir in the flour
    and cook for 2 minutes. Whisk in the milk and bring to the
    boil. Add the mustard, most of the breadcrumbs and most of
    the cheese. Stir until the sauce has thickened. Season with
    salt and pepper.

4. Tip the cauliflower into an ovenproof pan and pour
    the sauce over. Sprinkle with the remaining cheese and
    breadcrumbs.

5. Bake for 25 minutes, or until puffed and golden. Garnish
    with the dill, if desired.

Roast leg of lamb with 50 cloves of garlic

*'When I went to a railway station in Suffolk UK, on the menu
was this dish. I asked how to make it and was told it was a secret.
I said I was going to Australia, so no problem.' Tony Loades*

SERVES: 6–8

2 kg leg of lamb

50 garlic cloves, peeled

1½ cups white wine

1. Preheat the oven to 140°C. Brown the lamb in a large frying pan over medium heat. Place the lamb in a roasting pan and add the garlic cloves.

2. Pour in the wine and 1½ cups of water. Cover with foil or a very tight-fitting lid and roast for about 4 hours. Do not uncover during cooking.

3. Remove from the oven. Carve the meat if you can, it should fall to pieces (and you will hardly taste the garlic).

Clam chowder

A thicker variety than other chowders, this New England variety is a delicious seafood dish full of flavour and texture.

SERVES: 4

3 kg fresh clams (try your local fish market)

salt and pepper, to season

olive oil, as needed

2 garlic cloves, crushed

1 carrot, finely diced

1 celery stalk, finely diced

1 onion, finely diced

1 tablespoon thyme

2 bay leaves

450 g potatoes, peeled and cut into small cubes

100 g bacon, finely diced

1 cup thick cream

2 tablespoons finely chopped parsley, to serve

1. Soak the clams in a bowl of cold water with salt for 1 hour. Wash thoroughly.

2. Heat 2 tablespoons of olive oil in a large saucepan over medium heat. Add the garlic. Fold in the clams and cover with a lid. Allow to cook for about 10 minutes, until the shells open and the liquid is released. Remove the pan from the heat and discard the garlic.

3. Strain the clam liquid and set aside. Remove the clams from their shells.

4. Heat 1 tablespoon of olive oil in a large saucepan over medium heat. Add the carrot, celery, onion, thyme and bay leaves. Sauté this mixture for 5 minutes, stirring occasionally.

5. Add the potato and bacon to the saucepan and stir-fry for
   1 minute. Add the clam liquid and cover with a lid. Cook
   until the potato is soft.

6. Add the cream to the chowder and season with salt and
   pepper. Bring to the boil, then remove from the heat.
   Discard the bay leaves.

7. Blend the mixture until smooth and return to the heat. Add
   the clams to the pot. Serve hot with the parsley scattered on
   top.

Frankfurts, tomato and onion

'Fifty-three years ago, when I was still at home, my mother used to make this easy meal on Sunday evenings. My future husband enjoyed this with us and now he often says, let's have frankfurts tonight.' Carol Stumbles

SERVES: 2

1 tablespoon oil
1 onion, chopped
1 tomato, chopped

8 mini frankfurts, sliced
toast, to serve
tomato sauce, to serve

1. Heat the oil in a frying pan over medium heat. Add the onion and cook until lightly browned.

2. Add the tomato and frankfurts and cook for 3–4 minutes, or until the frankfurts are cooked through. Season.

3. Pour the mixture over pieces of toast, drizzle with the tomato sauce and enjoy.

Note: This is such an easy and enjoyable quick meal when in a hurry or on a lazy Sunday evening.

Lasagne

Comfort food at its best — all hail the classic lasagne. If you want to be the favourite at home with the family tonight, serve this to your loved ones for dinner. Delish!

SERVES: 6

2 teaspoons olive oil, plus extra
  to grease
1 onion, finely chopped
2 garlic cloves, crushed
750 g beef mince
2 x 400 g tins diced tomatoes
½ cup dry red wine
3 tablespoons tomato paste
salt and pepper, to season
4 fresh lasagne sheets
½ cup coarsely grated
  mozzarella cheese

Béchamel sauce
1 litre milk
1 onion, roughly chopped
8 parsley stalks
8 whole black peppercorns
4 whole cloves
2 bay leaves
60 g butter
⅓ cup plain flour
1 cup finely grated parmesan
  cheese
pinch of nutmeg
white pepper

1. Heat the oil in a frying pan over medium heat. Add the onion and garlic and cook, stirring, for 5 minutes, or until the onion softens.

2. Add the mince and cook, stirring with a wooden spoon to break up any lumps, for 5 minutes, or until the mince changes colour.

3. Add the tomato, wine and tomato paste and bring to the boil. Reduce the heat to low. Simmer, uncovered, stirring occasionally, for 30 minutes, or until the sauce thickens slightly. Remove from the heat. Season with salt and pepper.

4. Meanwhile, make the béchamel sauce. Combine the milk, onion, parsley stalks, peppercorns, cloves and bay leaves in a saucepan and bring to a simmer over medium heat. Remove from the heat and set aside for 15 minutes to infuse.

5. Strain the milk mixture through a fine sieve into a large jug. Discard the solids.

6. Melt the butter in a large saucepan over medium–high heat until foaming. Add the flour and cook, stirring, for 1–2 minutes, or until the mixture bubbles and begins to come away from the side of the pan. Remove from the heat.

7. Gradually pour in half the milk, whisking constantly with a balloon whisk, until the mixture is smooth. Gradually add the remaining milk, whisking until smooth and combined.

8. Place the saucepan over medium–high heat and bring to the boil, stirring constantly with a wooden spoon, for 5 minutes, or until the sauce thickens and coats the back of the spoon. Remove from the heat. Add the parmesan and stir until the cheese melts. Taste and season with the nutmeg, salt and white pepper.

9. Preheat the oven to 180°C. Lightly grease a rectangular 3 litre ovenproof dish with oil.

10. Spread a quarter of the béchamel sauce over the base of the prepared dish. Arrange one lasagne sheet over the sauce. Top with one-third of the mince mixture and one-third of the remaining béchamel sauce. Continue layering with the remaining lasagne sheets, mince mixture and béchamel, finishing with a layer of béchamel. Sprinkle with the mozzarella. Place on a baking tray and bake for 40 minutes, or until the cheese melts, is golden brown, and the edges are bubbling. Remove from the oven and set aside for 10 minutes to set.

Cod pie

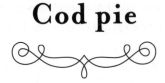

'My mother used to make this on a monthly basis and I've now started baking it too. My husband's English and a fussy eater, but he loves it. It's extremely easy to make and looks good and is amazingly tasty! It's a "no-fail" recipe.' Helen Woodward

SERVES: 2–3

2 potatoes, peeled and chopped

30 g butter

1 egg, beaten

Filling

2 small pieces smoked cod

1 tablespoon butter

1 tablespoon plain flour

1 cup milk

1 celery stalk, chopped

2 spring onions, chopped

¼ cup grated tasty cheese

1 tablespoon grated parmesan cheese

1 tablespoon parsley, chopped

1. Preheat the oven to 160°C. Lightly grease a casserole dish.

2. Boil and mash the potatoes. Add the butter and egg and mix well. Spoon into the prepared dish and press slightly up the sides of the dish. Bake for 5 minutes, then remove from the oven.

3. Meanwhile, for the filling, simmer the cod in a large saucepan of boiling water for 5 minutes. Drain and flake with a fork.

4. Melt the butter in a saucepan over medium heat, Add the flour, milk, celery, spring onion and tasty cheese. Gently mix in the flaked cod.

5. Spoon the fish mixture into the part-baked potato shell and sprinkle the parmesan and parsley on top. Bake for 35 minutes.

Baked eggplant

*Hearty, delicious and nutritious, this dish isn't completely
guilt free but it's not as bad as its carb-laden relatives.*

SERVES: 8

2 tablespoons oil

2 large eggs

¾ cup plain dry breadcrumbs

¾ cup finely grated parmesan
cheese, plus extra 2
tablespoons for topping

1 teaspoon dried oregano

½ teaspoon dried basil

salt and pepper, to season

2 large eggplants, peeled and
sliced into 1 cm rounds

1.5 litres store-bought or
homemade chunky tomato
sauce

1½ cups shredded mozzarella
cheese

1. Preheat the oven to 180°C. Lightly grease two baking trays
    with oil and set aside.

2. In a bowl, whisk together the eggs and 2 tablespoons of
    water.

3. In another bowl, combine the breadcrumbs, ¾ cup
    parmesan cheese, oregano and basil and season with salt and
    pepper.

4. Dip the eggplant slices in the egg mixture, allow the excess
    to drip off and then coat well in the breadcrumb mixture.
    Place on the baking trays.

5. Bake the eggplant for 20–25 minutes, or until golden brown. Turn the slices and continue baking for a further 20–25 minutes, or until browned. Remove from the oven. Increase the oven temperature to 200°C.

6. Spread 2 cups of the tomato sauce in a baking dish. Arrange half the eggplant in the dish and cover with 2 cups of sauce. Top with ½ cup mozzarella. Repeat with the remaining eggplant, sauce and mozzarella. Sprinkle with the 2 tablespoons of parmesan cheese.

7. Bake for 15–20 minutes, or until the sauce is bubbling and the cheese is melted. Leave to stand for 5 minutes before serving.

Mum's sweet brisket

'After the war my mother was always on a tight budget and so nourishing recipes that were also cheap to make were high on her agenda. She was always worried we'd get scurvy and served boiled nettles with the silverbeet. But this brisket was the favourite of my sisters and I. My mum was a clever cook, she'd crush a couple of Weet-Bix into the rissoles to make them go further but still be nourishing. Our school sandwiches were always meat and salad (which we'd swap for jam or baked bean sandwiches). I'm 70 and still using her recipes.' Valerie O'Doherty

SERVES: 4

1 tablespoon vegetable oil
2 kg piece beef brisket
2 onions, halved and sliced
  into wedges
1 kg waxy potatoes, peeled and
  thickly sliced

400 g pitted prunes
salt and pepper, to season
175 g golden syrup
2 tablespoons lemon juice

1. Heat the oil in a saucepan large enough to hold the brisket. Add the brisket and brown the brisket on all sides.

2. Add the onion, potato, three-quarters of the prunes and 2 teaspoons of salt. Cover with boiling water and half of the golden syrup. Bring to the boil, partially cover, then simmer for at least 1 hour 30 minutes, or until quite tender.

3. Preheat the oven to 180°C. Remove the meat from the pan and place in an ovenproof dish. Strain and reserve the liquid and spoon the onion, potato and prunes on top of the brisket. Pour enough liquid into the dish so that it comes halfway up the meat. Top with the remaining prunes and golden syrup. Sprinkle over ½ teaspoon of salt and plenty of pepper.

4. Roast, uncovered, basting every 15 minutes or so, for 1 hour–1 hour 30 minutes, or until the meat is fork tender. To serve, sprinkle with the lemon juice.

Easy lentil stew

*This hearty vegetarian stew not only packs a flavour punch
but it's so easy to make — it's all done in one-pot!*

SERVES: 4

1 cup dry lentils

3 cups vegetable stock

1 x 400 g tin peeled Italian
   tomatoes

1 cup diced potatoes

1 cup chopped carrots

1 onion, sliced

2 garlic cloves, minced

1 tablespoon dried basil

1 tablespoon dried parsley

salt and pepper, to season

chopped parsley, to garnish

crusty bread, to serve

1. Combine all the ingredients, except the fresh parsley,
    together in a saucepan over medium heat.

2. Simmer for 45 minutes, or until the lentils and vegetables
    are tender. Stir occasionally.

3. Remove from the heat and garnish with the parsley. Serve
    warm with crusty bread.

Apricot chicken

'This was passed to me when I was in the Junior League in Charlotte NC. We actually developed our own cookbook and this recipe is one that I have used frequently for the family as well as dinner parties. It always brings compliments.' Barbara Holmes

SERVES: 8

8 chicken breast fillets
1 x 410 g tin apricots, drained
1 tablespoon butter

1 x 40 g packet French onion
  soup mix
white or wild rice, steamed, to
  serve

1. Preheat the oven to 160°C. Place the chicken breasts in a baking dish. Place the apricots on top of the chicken. Dot the butter on the apricots. Sprinkle the onion soup mix over the top.

2. Cover the baking dish with foil. Bake for 1 hour 30 minutes, then uncover and bake for a further 30 minutes to brown. Serve over steamed white or wild rice.

Traditional meatloaf

For a meal that is sure to delight the entire family — from young to old — the trusty old meatloaf is a winner every time.

SERVES: 8

I tablespoon olive oil

I large onion, finely chopped

3 garlic cloves, crushed

I cup fresh breadcrumbs

3 tablespoons milk

2 tablespoons finely chopped rosemary

I tablespoon dijon mustard

2 eggs

400 g pork mince

400 g veal mince

½ cup chopped pancetta

salt and pepper, to season

1. Preheat the oven to 180°C. Lightly grease a loaf tin.

2. Heat the oil in a non-stick frying pan over medium heat. Add the onion and garlic and cook for 5–7 minutes, or until softened. Allow to cool completely.

3. Place the breadcrumbs and milk in a large bowl and set aside for 5 minutes, or until the milk is absorbed.

4. Add the onion mixture, the rosemary, mustard, eggs, pork and veal mince and pancetta. Season with salt and pepper and mix well to combine.

5. Press the mixture into the loaf tin. Place the tin on a baking tray and bake for 40–45 minutes, or until just cooked. Set aside for 5 minutes before inverting onto a tray lined with non-stick baking paper. Bake for a further 5–10 minutes, or until golden.

Corned silverside

'This recipe was handed down from my wife's side of the family of English/Scottish origin. Her parents migrated to Australia in 1956, the year I was born. I have taken their recipe to my heart and my wife always loved it except that she had to make the white sauce.' Barry Meyer

SERVES: 4–8 (DEPENDING ON SIZE OF MEAT)

corned beef, preferably eye-cut
1 onion, skin on
1 tablespoon dark brown sugar
1 tablespoon wholegrain
  mustard

6 whole cloves
1 teaspoon whole black
  peppercorns
½ cup malt vinegar

1. Place the meat in a 6 litre pot along with the remaining ingredients. Fill the pot with cold water and heat to a slow simmer. Ensure the water does not bubble vigorously (cooking too fast causes the meat to become stringy). Depending on the size of the meat, it will take 2–3 hours of slow simmering to bring the meat to the top, indicating it is ready. (You can always check with a thermometer — 74°C should be just right.)

2. Remove the meat from the liquid and cover with foil. Rest for at least 15–20 minutes before serving.

3. Serve with mashed potato, carrots, beans and peas along with a white sauce over the meat (cooked onion or celery in the sauce is the perfect addition).

Note: Pickled pork can be cooked the same way but I use cider vinegar, and drop the mustard and cloves. A hot apple sauce goes well with the pork.

Bubble-and-squeak croquettes

Turn leftover veggies into these delectable crispy, golden croquettes of goodness. The family will love them!

SERVES: 6

25 g butter
200 g bacon, trimmed, chopped
6 cups finely chopped mixed vegetables (choose your favourites — cabbage, corn, peas and spring onions work well)
1 handful herbs, such as parsley or mint

3 cups mashed starchy vegetables, such as potato, sweet potato and pumpkin
salt and pepper
1 egg
4 tablespoons milk
¾ cup plain flour
1 cup fine dried breadcrumbs
extra-light olive oil, to shallow-fry
lemon wedges, to serve

1. Melt the butter in a large non-stick frying pan over medium heat. Add the bacon and cook, stirring occasionally, for 2 minutes, or until golden. Add the mixed veggies and cook, stirring occasionally, for 4 minutes, or until soft. Transfer to a large bowl.

2. Add the herbs and mashed veggies to the bowl. Season to taste and mix well to combine.

3. Use damp hands to roll 2 tablespoonfuls of the mixture into 7 cm long croquettes. Place on a baking tray lined with baking paper. Refrigerate for 20 minutes, or until firm.

4. Whisk the egg and milk together in a shallow bowl. Place the flour and breadcrumbs in separate bowls. Roll each croquette in the flour and shake off any excess. Dip in the egg, then in the breadcrumbs to coat. Place on a baking tray lined with baking paper.

5. Add the oil to a large non-stick frying pan and heat over medium–high heat. Shallow-fry the croquettes, in batches, turning, for 2 minutes, or until golden brown. Drain on paper towels. Season and serve with the lemon wedges.

Lambs fry and bacon

'My mother cut up lambs fry like stir-fry and I loved the taste. I joined the army at 18 and was taught to cook. On my first leave at home, I offered to cook dinner, serving lambs fry and bacon. My father told my mother that it was the best lambs fry that she ever made!' Maree Johnson

SERVES: 4

2 tablespoons oil
1 light lambs fry, skinned,
   thinly sliced
6 bacon rashers, rind removed,
   chopped into small pieces

1 large onion, chopped
3 tablespoons plain flour
salt, to taste

1. Heat the oil in a deep frying pan over medium heat and fry the lamb slices in batches until brown (do not overcook). Remove from the pan and keep warm.

2. Add the bacon to the pan and cook until beginning to crisp. Remove from the pan and keep warm.

3. Add the onion to the pan and cook until browned. Add the flour to make a roux and cook until brown, stirring to avoid any lumps. Remove from the heat and add 2 cups of water, stirring constantly to remove any lumps.

4. Return the pan to the heat and add the lambs fry and bacon. Season to taste. Bring to the boil, then simmer for 5–10 minutes. Serve with mashed potato and peas, or over toast.

Note 1: It's important to make sure you slice the lambs fry very thinly. I cut it like I was skinning a fish.

Note 2: This recipe can be frozen in batches and reheated.

Cheese-stuffed zucchini flowers

An easy, tasty vegetarian entrée that will be sure to impress guests.

SERVES: 2 (AS AN ENTRÉE)

100 g ricotta cheese

20 g gorgonzola cheese, crumbled

20 g parmesan cheese, finely grated, plus 1 tablespoon extra, to serve

salt and pepper, to season

1 egg

6 zucchini flowers

vegetable oil, for deep-frying

450 ml cold soda water

250 g plain flour

1. Combine the ricotta, gorgonzola and parmesan in a bowl. Season with salt and pepper. Add the egg and mix well.

2. Carefully open the zucchini flower petals. Remove the stamen or pistil.

3. Cut the corner of a freezer bag to make a piping bag. Add the cheese mixture to the bag and pipe the mixture into the flower. Twist the petals to enclose the filling.

4. Heat the vegetable oil in a saucepan or deep-fryer. To test if the oil is hot enough, dip the back of a wooden spoon in the oil to see if bubbles appear.

5. While the oil is heating, whisk the soda water and flour in a bowl.

6. Dip a stuffed zucchini flower in the batter, letting the excess batter drip off, and fry immediately in the hot oil. Repeat with the remaining zucchini flowers.

7. Sprinkle with the extra grated parmesan and serve warm.

Poached salmon

*'It's our favourite home-cooked salmon recipe which
I have been making for years.' Vicki Engel*

SERVES: 2

1 cup freshly squeezed juice
  (orange and/or mandarin)

2 salmon fillets
lemon pepper

1. Pour the juice into a non-stick frying pan and place the salmon fillets in the pan. Sprinkle with the lemon pepper.

2. Bring the juice to the boil and cook over high heat, turning the fillets once after 3–5 minutes. Sprinkle the other side of the salmon with lemon pepper.

3. Continue cooking until the sauce has thickened and reduced in volume. Remove the salmon from the pan and place on two serving plates. Pour the sauce over the salmon fillets and serve.

Note: The salmon goes well served with avocado salsa or topped with garlic prawns, and a selection of colourful cooked vegetables or a salad.

Classic moussaka

For a casserole with a difference, try our take on the signature Mediterranean dish — we promise it's as hearty as it looks.

SERVES: 4

2 large eggplants, thinly sliced
salt and pepper, to season
olive oil, for shallow-frying
1 onion, finely chopped
3 garlic cloves, crushed
500 g lamb mince
1 x 400 g tin crushed tomatoes
4 tablespoons tomato paste
¼ teaspoon cinnamon

1 teaspoon caster sugar
⅓ cup grated cheddar cheese
lemon wedges, to serve
Béchamel sauce
60 g butter
¼ cup plain flour
2 cups milk
4 tablespoon grated parmesan
  cheese

1. Salt the eggplant slices on both sides and rest for 1 hour.

2. Preheat the oven to 180°C. Rinse the eggplant slices with cold water and pat the slices dry. Brush the eggplant slices with olive oil and cook in a frying pan over high heat until lightly browned. Set aside.

3. Heat 2 tablespoons of oil in the frying pan and sauté the onion and garlic for 5 minutes, or until the onion has softened. Add the mince and cook, stirring, for 6–8 minutes, or until browned. Add the tomatoes, tomato paste, cinnamon and sugar. Bring to the boil. Reduce the heat to medium–low and simmer for 30 minutes, or until the sauce is thick and the liquid evaporated. Season to taste.

4. To make the béchamel sauce, heat the butter in a saucepan over medium heat and add the flour. Stir over low heat for 2–3 minutes, or until the mixture is bubbling. Gradually add the milk and stir until the mixture starts to boil and thicken. Stir in the parmesan and season to taste.

5. Grease a large ovenproof dish and layer one-third of the eggplant slices, slightly overlapping, over the base. Spread half of the meat mixture over the eggplant. Repeat the layers, finishing with the eggplant. Spread the béchamel sauce over. Sprinkle with the grated cheddar cheese. Bake for 30 minutes, or until golden. Serve with the lemon wedges.

Broccoli chicken

'Joyce, who is now 92, gave me this recipe when we were neighbours and I was a young mum of three young children. I was looking for a tasty, healthy, easy and economical family recipe. This one ticked all the boxes and I am 70 now and still use it frequently, as do my children who are 35, 33 and 31. We have shared this recipe with many of our friends and neighbours and it has become a favourite to take to share at gatherings.' Marie Hills

SERVES: 5

350 g broccoli
500 g chicken breast fillets
1 x 400 g tin chicken and
  mushroom soup
1 teaspoon curry powder

½ cup mayonnaise
¾ cup milk
3 tablespoons dry breadcrumbs
4 tablespoons grated cheese

1. Preheat the oven to 180°C. Lightly steam the broccoli and place in a casserole dish.

2. Lightly steam the chicken breast fillets and cut into strips. Place the chicken over the broccoli.

3. Combine the soup, curry powder, mayonnaise and milk in a large bowl. Pour the mixture into the casserole dish.

4. Sprinkle the breadcrumbs and grated cheese over the chicken mixture. Bake for 30–45 minutes, or until the chicken is cooked. Serve with rice, mashed potato, carrots or pumpkin.

The Way Mum Made It

Time to celebrate

*'My way of communicating love and interest in people
is through cooking. I grew up in an environment where
food was really celebrated, and that gave me the message:
food makes people happy.'*
— Kylie Kwong

There's nothing quite like gathering loved ones around
the dinner table — or even for a little stand-up cocktail
soiree — to celebrate Christmas. In fact, any excuse
for a celebration generally means hearts are warm with
love, rooms are full of laughter and bellies are satisfied
from tables of decadent food. Is there any better way to
celebrate? From birthdays to holidays, we have all of your
occasions wrapped up with this chapter full of old-school
dishes, Australian favourites and some family secrets.

Sparkling punch

Grandpa Blue

MAKES: 20 GLASSES

½ cup sugar
juice of 1 orange
juice of 1 lemon
juice of 1 grapefruit
1 x 375 ml tin pineapple juice
1 cup brandy

500 ml bottle Morello cherry
   cordial, chilled
1½ bottles Champagne or
   sparkling wine, chilled
1 x 1.25 litre bottle soda water,
   chilled

1. Combine the sugar, juices and brandy in a large bowl or jug.
    Refrigerate for several hours.

2. When ready to serve, add the well-chilled Morello cherry
    cordial, Champagne or sparkling wine and soda water.

Prawn cocktails

If there's one thing we look forward to during summer it is gorgeous seafood. There's nothing quite better than an ice-cold wine and delicious summer prawns on a hot day. Whether it's for a family lunch or an entrée for Christmas, this is a go-to summer recipe.

MAKES: 4

1 iceberg lettuce, shredded
600 g cooked prawns, peeled
sweet paprika, to garnish
Cocktail sauce
3 tablespoons tomato sauce

3 tablespoons pouring cream
1 tablespoon lemon juice
1 teaspoon worcestershire sauce
dash of Tabasco sauce
salt and pepper, to season

1. To make the cocktail sauce, combine the tomato sauce, cream, lemon juice, worcestershire sauce and Tabasco sauce in a small bowl. Season with salt and pepper.

2. Place the lettuce in four cocktail glasses. Top with the prawns, drizzle with the cocktail sauce and garnish with the paprika. Serve immediately.

Boiled fruitcake

'This recipe was given to me by a lady I worked for when I was 15 years old. I have no idea how many times I have made it. When we had our business, I would make several at Christmas time and give them to our employees and clients.' Hazel Lowery

SERVES: 20

115 g unsalted butter
¾ cup sugar
460 g mixed fruit
1 teaspoon mixed spice
1 teaspoon nutmeg
1 teaspoon bicarbonate of soda
2 eggs, beaten

1 cup plain flour, sifted
1 cup self-raising flour, sifted
1 teaspoon lemon extract
1 teaspoon vanilla extract
2 tablespoons dark rum
  (optional)

1. Place the butter, sugar, fruit, spice, nutmeg, bicarbonate of soda and 1 cup of water in a saucepan and bring to the boil. Simmer for 15 minutes, stirring occasionally. Allow to cool — preferably overnight.

2. Preheat the oven to 180°C. Lightly grease a 20 cm round cake tin and line with baking paper.

3. Add the well-beaten eggs and sifted flours to the fruit mixture. Add the lemon extract, vanilla and rum (if using). Mix well to combine.

4. Pour the mixture into the prepared tin and bake for 1 hour, or until a skewer inserted into the centre comes out clean. Leave to cool in the tin for 5 minutes, then turn out onto a wire rack to cool completely.

Note: This recipe is great on its own, spread with butter or warmed and covered in custard.

Warm potato salad

*When loved ones gather around for celebrations why not
mix things up with a warm take on this summer classic.*

SERVES: 6

1 kg small new potatoes, halved
2 tablespoons olive oil
4 bacon rashers, diced
3 tablespoons whole-egg
mayonnaise

1 tablespoon lemon juice
2 teaspoons dijon mustard
salt and pepper, to season
1 handful chopped rosemary

1. Bring a large pot of water to the boil and cook the potatoes
    until tender. Drain and set aside in a large heatproof bowl to
    cool slightly.

2. Heat 1 tablespoon of the oil in a frying pan over medium
    heat. Add the bacon and cook until crispy. Pour the bacon
    (and any juice or fat from the pan) into the bowl with the
    potatoes and toss to combine.

3. Whisk the remaining olive oil, the mayonnaise, lemon juice,
    dijon mustard, and salt and pepper together and drizzle over
    the salad. Scatter with the chopped rosemary and serve.

Pavlova

Nothing signals a celebration more than a pavlova. Treat the family with this recipe that is sure to see you serve up a perfectly cooked pav.

Perfect pavlova tips

If you want to ensure your pavlova rises, doesn't sink and is the perfect texture, here are some handy hints for perfecting the recipe...

- Make sure your whisking bowl is clean. Give it a light wash with vinegar before use.

- Have everything ready on the bench. When you start mixing the pavlova, you should not stop for anything.

- Make sure the eggs are as fresh as possible.

- The egg whites must not contain any trace of yolk. Separate the eggs individually and bring the whites to room temperature.

- You can use the yolks to make a delicious custard to go with the pav.

SERVES: 8

6 egg whites
1½ cups caster sugar
1 tablespoon cornflour, sifted
1½ cups thickened cream
1 tablespoon icing sugar
1 teaspoon vanilla extract

250 g strawberries, hulled and
   halved, to decorate
150 g blueberries, to decorate
⅓ cup fresh passionfruit pulp,
   to decorate

1. Preheat the oven to 150°C. Cut out a 23–29 cm circle with baking paper. Place the circle on a baking tray.

2. Using an electric mixer, beat the egg whites in a large bowl until soft peaks form. Gradually add the caster sugar, beating until dissolved and scraping down the side of the bowl occasionally. Use a large metal spoon or spatula to fold in the sifted cornflour.

3. Spoon the mixture onto the prepared baking paper on the tray. Use a metal spatula or the back of a spoon to spread the meringue into a circle.

4. Bake the pavlova in the lower half of the oven for 1 hour 30 minutes, or until dry and crisp. Turn off the oven. Leave to cool in the oven with the door slightly ajar.

5. Using the electric mixer, beat the cream, icing sugar and vanilla until soft peaks form.

6. Place the pavlova on a serving plate. Top with the cream mixture and fruit (you can really use any fruit you like here). Serve immediately.

Note: Although it's best to make the pavlova up to a day before you serve it, the base will keep for up to two days in an airtight container at room temperature. Don't refrigerate it as it will lose its crunchy texture.

The Way Mum Made It

Satay chicken in lettuce cups

'I found the idea for this recipe in a Saturday morning paper but have adapted it for my family. It's requested by my grandchildren when they come to visit and hubby loves it as well! Actually my grandson, Brayden, told his mum that I served this delicious chicken stuff in lettuce and said, "I know why you are such a cook — you take after Nanna!"' Marilyn Hulslander

SERVES: 4 (OR MORE IF SERVED AS AN ENTRÉE)

2 tablespoons olive oil

500 g chicken mince

½ red capsicum, cut into strips

½ green capsicum, cut into strips

1 onion, quartered and cut downwards into strips

2–3 cups chicken stock

100 g Thai rice noodles

iceberg lettuce leaves (go for outer leaves if serving as a main or smaller leaves if serving as an entrée)

1 spring onion, chopped, to garnish

4 tablespoons sweet chilli sauce, to serve

Thai satay paste

2 tablespoons peanut butter

2 limes, juiced

1 tablespoon coriander paste

3 tablespoons fish sauce

2 teaspoons minced garlic

2 teaspoons minced ginger

2 teaspoons minced chilli

1. To make the Thai satay paste, mix all of the ingredients together.

2. Heat the oil in a large frying pan over medium heat. Add the chicken and cook for 10 minutes, breaking up any lumps during cooking.

3. Add the capsicums and onion and cook for 5 minutes. Stir in the Thai satay paste and cook, stirring, for 5 minutes.

4. Add half the stock and stir in. Break up the rice noodles and add to the pan. Continue stirring and add more chicken stock as needed to hydrate the noodles. The mixture should be firm and the noodles fully cooked.

5. To serve, put the lettuce leaves on a serving plate. Spoon the chicken mixture on top and garnish with the chopped spring onion. Serve with the sweet chilli sauce on the side.

Note: Chicken stock is added to just hydrate the noodles. Be careful not to add too much.

Tiramisu

Tiramisu is such a decadent and elegant dessert to finish any dinner. What's great about this recipe is that you can make your own individual servings (a tiraminisu, if you will) — no need to spend time in the kitchen dishing out individual portions. Just place these in front of your guests and enjoy yourself. Adjust these quantities based on the size of your serving glasses.

SERVES: 4

100 ml espresso (or very strong instant coffee)
2 tablespoons coffee liqueur
2 large egg whites
250 g mascarpone cheese
2 tablespoons honey

2 tablespoons Marsala
6 sponge finger biscuits, plus 2 extra sponge fingers, halved
unsweetened cocoa powder, to dust

1. Make your espresso (or instant coffee) and add the coffee liqueur. Leave this aside in a heatproof jug to cool.

2. Using an electric mixer, beat the egg whites until soft peaks form.

3. In a separate bowl, using an electric mixer, beat the mascarpone with the honey until smooth. Beat in the Marsala.

4. Fold the egg whites into the mascarpone mix, a third at a time.

5. Prepare four glass tumblers or stemless wine glasses. Spoon a little of the mascarpone mixture into the bottom of each glass. Then break the sponge fingers into quarters and dip them in the espresso and liqueur, allowing them to soak it up. Lay these on top of the mascarpone and pour any excess coffee over the top. Cover the biscuits using the rest of the mascarpone mixture.

6. Dust the tops with the cocoa power (push it through a sieve for best results) and serve with half a sponge finger sticking out the top. Refrigerate until ready to serve.

Jerk chicken drumsticks

SERVES: 4–6

1.5 kg chicken drumsticks
salt and pepper, to season
1 lime, cut into wedges, to serve
Jerk marinade
1 onion, chopped
2 garlic cloves, finely chopped
2 teaspoons finely grated ginger
3 habanero chillies, seeded, chopped

2 tablespoons vegetable oil
½ cup lime juice
2 tablespoons sugar
2 tablespoons thyme
1 tablespoon rosemary
1 tablespoon ground allspice
2 teaspoons cinnamon
½ teaspoon nutmeg

1. To make the jerk marinade, place all the ingredients in a blender and pulse until a paste forms. Rub the paste over the chicken, cover and refrigerate overnight.

2. Preheat the barbecue grill to medium–high. Season the chicken with salt and pepper. Cook, turning, for 20 minutes, or until the chicken is cooked through.

3. Serve the chicken with the lime wedges.

Lamingtons

*There's a reason this recipe is an Aussie favourite — it's
hard to resist the light and fluffy much-loved classic.*

SERVES: 20

4 eggs
⅔ cup caster sugar
I cup self-raising flour
¼ cup cornflour
25 g unsalted butter, chopped
4 tablespoons boiling water
3 cups desiccated coconut

Chocolate icing
⅔ cup icing sugar mixture
½ cup unsweetened cocoa
   powder
20 g soft unsalted butter
¾ cup milk

1. Preheat the oven to 180°C. Grease and flour a 20 cm x
    30 cm lamington tin and line the base with baking paper.

2. Using an electric mixer, beat the eggs in a small bowl
    until light in colour. Gradually add the sugar, beating for
    8 minutes, or until the mixture is thick.

3. Meanwhile, sift the flour and cornflour together three
    times. Combine the butter and boiling water in a small
    heatproof bowl.

4. Transfer the egg mixture to a large bowl. Sift the flour
    mixture over the egg mixture. Using a balloon whisk or a
    large metal spoon, gently fold the flour into the egg mixture,
    then fold in the butter mixture.

The Way Mum Made It

5. Pour the mixture into the prepared tin. Bake for 25 minutes, or until the sponge springs back when touched lightly in the centre and comes away from the side of the tin. Turn the cake onto a wire rack to cool.

6. Cut the cooled cake into 20 even pieces.

7. To make the chocolate icing, sift the icing sugar and cocoa powder into a large heatproof bowl. Add the butter and milk and stir over a saucepan of simmering water until the icing is smooth and thick enough to coat the back of a spoon. Divide the icing mixture into two small bowls.

8. Place the coconut in a shallow bowl.

9. Using a large fork, dip each piece of cake briefly into the icing until the cake is coated. Hold over the bowl to drain off any excess. Dip half the cake pieces in one bowl of icing and the other half in the second bowl of icing. (If the icing becomes too thick, stand it over hot water while dipping, or reheat gently with a touch more milk. If necessary, strain the icing into a clean bowl.)

10. Toss the cake gently in the coconut. Transfer the cake to a wire rack to set.

Note: The cake is easier to handle if it is made a day ahead or refrigerated for several hours.

Rhubarb champagne

'My grandmother made this in the 1940s. My mum made it in the '70s. Now I make it. It's a very old recipe that brings back such special memories of my nan and mum.' Jan Caine

MAKES: 3.75 LITRES

900 g rhubarb, cut into small
  pieces
2 tablespoons vinegar

2 lemons, thinly sliced
680 g white sugar

1. Combine all of the ingredients with 3.75 litres of water in a large plastic container or bucket and stir well. Cover with muslin cloth and leave for 2 days.

2. Strain into bottles and cork.

Note: The flavour improves with age.

Cheesy potato bake

*The perfect accompaniment to any meal, everyone
needs a great potato bake recipe in his or her repertoire
and this one is delicious (and simple).*

SERVES: 6

60 g butter, plus extra, melted,
   for greasing
2⅓ cups milk
400 ml pouring cream
2 cups grated tasty cheese

1.5 kg potatoes (sebago, desiree,
   or similar), peeled and thinly
   sliced
1 onion, finely chopped
3 garlic cloves, crushed
1 tablespoon thyme leaves
salt and pepper, to season

1. Preheat the oven to 180°C. Lightly grease a 1.75 litre
   ovenproof dish.

2. Melt the butter in a heavy-based saucepan over medium heat.
   Slowly add the milk and cream, stirring constantly until well
   combined. Add 1½ cups of cheese. Stir to combine.

3. Layer one-third of the potato over the base of the dish,
   overlapping slightly. Top with half the onion, garlic, thyme
   and one-third of the cheese sauce. Season with salt and
   pepper. Repeat, finishing with a layer of potato.

4. Brush a sheet of foil with oil and place oil-side down over the potato. Seal tightly. Bake for 45 minutes. Uncover and brush the top with the melted butter. Cook for a further 45 minutes, or until tender and golden brown. Sprinkle with the remaining cheese for the remaining 15 minutes of cooking.

Kill me quicks

'My mother cooked this recipe for parties and guests for many years. I don't know where she got it from or who devised the name, but it was always a hit with our family and visitors. I've been using it for over 40 years and she must have used it for at least as long. These days I avoid making them as I am tempted to eat the lot!' Kaye Ambrose

MAKES: ABOUT 20

3 egg whites
1½ cups sugar

1½ cups crushed cornflakes

1. Preheat the oven to 180°C. Lightly grease a baking tray.

2. Using an electric mixer, beat the egg whites and sugar together until stiff. Add the cornflakes and fold to combine.

3. Spoon teaspoon-sized amounts of the mixture onto the prepared tray. Bake for 10–15 minutes.

Note: Serve individually with cream on top or join together with cream in between.

Chicken satay skewers

For a meal that the entire family will enjoy — from young to old — these chicken skewers should be your go-to. Serve with rice and a cucumber salad for a refreshing and healthy dinner.

SERVES: 3–4

600 g chicken breast fillets

1 lemongrass stalk, white part only, finely chopped

2 teaspoons finely grated ginger

1 tablespoon light soy sauce

1 teaspoon ground coriander

1 teaspoon ground cumin

½ teaspoon turmeric

2 tablespoons finely chopped palm sugar

½ cup toasted peanuts, finely chopped

1 x 270 ml tin coconut milk

1 tablespoon lime juice

1 tablespoon fish sauce

12 bamboo skewers, soaked in water for 15 minutes

½ cup coriander leaves, to serve

1. Use a large sharp knife to cut through each chicken breast crossways. Cut lengthways into thirds and place in a large glass or ceramic bowl.

2. Combine the lemongrass, ginger, soy sauce, ground coriander, cumin, turmeric and 2 teaspoons of the palm sugar in a small bowl. Add half the paste to the chicken. Toss to coat and set aside for 15 minutes to develop the flavours.

3. Meanwhile, place the remaining paste, the peanuts and coconut milk in a saucepan over medium–low heat. Stir for 5 minutes, or until the sauce thickens and is heated through. Add the lime juice, fish sauce and remaining palm sugar and stir to combine. Taste and season further with extra lime juice or sugar, if desired.

4. Heat a barbecue or chargrill pan on medium heat. Thread the chicken evenly among the skewers. Cook for 2 minutes on each side, or until golden brown and cooked through. Remove from the heat.

5. Drizzle the chicken skewers with the peanut sauce and serve with the coriander leaves scattered on top.

Chocolate brownie cake

'Can't remember who or where the recipe came from, but it has been one of my family and friends' favourites that has been continually requested for 40-odd years.' Lorraine Delaney

SERVES: 6–8

dry breadcrumbs
1¼ cups sugar
⅔ cup plain flour
4 tablespoons unsweetened
  cocoa powder
¼ teaspoon salt

90 g unsalted butter, melted
  and cooled
2 eggs, beaten
1 teaspoon vanilla extract
½ cup flaked almonds

1. Preheat the oven to 170°C. Grease a 23 cm loose-based flan tin or springform cake tin. Sprinkle lightly with the breadcrumbs to coat.

2. Stir together the sugar, flour, cocoa and salt in a bowl and mix well.

3. Add the cooled butter, the eggs and vanilla and beat well.

4. Spoon the batter into the prepared tin and spread evenly. Sprinkle the top with the flaked almonds.

5. Bake on the lower shelf of the oven for 35 minutes, or until crusty on top but still moist in the middle. Set aside to cool and remove the side of the tin.

Note: Delicious served with plain cream, whipped cream, or ice cream and fresh berries. If it lasts — which it usually doesn't — it keeps well.

Garlic and parmesan roasted pumpkin

This simple side dish makes use of the sweet, nutty taste of butternut pumpkin, combining it with the irresistible flavours of garlic and parmesan.

SERVES: 6–8 (AS A SIDE DISH)

500 g butternut pumpkin, cut up into small chunks
4 tablespoons butter, melted
3 garlic cloves, minced

1 tablespoon finely chopped parsley leaves
salt and pepper, to season
⅓ cup grated parmesan cheese

1. Preheat the oven to 200°C. Line a baking tray with baking paper.

2. Toss the pumpkin pieces with the butter, garlic, parsley and salt and pepper. Spread the pumpkin in a single layer on the prepared tray.

3. Roast the pumpkin for about 40 minutes until a light brown colour and soft. Remove from the oven.

4. Sprinkle the parmesan cheese over the pumpkin and place in the still-warm oven until the cheese has melted. Serve immediately.

Anzac biscuits

'This is my grandmother's recipe for Anzac biscuits. Her name was Mary Sara Cecilia Saville and she was born in the late 1800s. This recipe was passed down to her daughter Joan (my great-grandmother) who was born in 1919 who then passed it on to her daughter Pamela (my grandma) born in 1948.' Pamela Morgan

MAKES: 20

1 cup plain flour
1 cup caster sugar
1 cup rolled oats
1 cup desiccated coconut
125 g unsalted butter

1 tablespoon golden syrup or treacle
2 tablespoons boiling water
1 teaspoon bicarbonate of soda

1. Preheat the oven to 180°C. Lightly grease two baking trays.

2. Combine the flour in a large bowl with the sugar, rolled oats and coconut.

3. Melt the butter and golden syrup in a saucepan over low heat.

4. Combine the boiling water with the bicarbonate of soda and stir to dissolve. Add to the butter mixture and mix well, then stir into the dry ingredients until thoroughly combined.

5. Drop teaspoons of the mixture onto the trays, allowing room for spreading. Bake for 10 minutes, or until golden brown. Allow to cool on the tray for a few minutes before transferring to a wire rack to cool.

Cheese fondue

Looking for something delicious and different to cook
for dinner? Try this simple old-school favourite.

SERVES: 4–6

1 cup white wine
1 garlic clove, crushed
1⅔ cups grated gruyère cheese
1⅔ cups grated cheddar cheese
½ cup mascarpone cheese
1–2 tablespoons kirsch

1–2 tablespoons boiling water
woodfired bread, brushed
  with olive oil, toasted or
  chargrilled, and cut into
  pieces

1. Place the wine and garlic in a saucepan over medium–low
   heat and cook for 5–6 minutes, or until reduced by half.

2. Add the gruyère and cheddar cheeses and melt, stirring
   occasionally, until smooth and combined.

3. When ready to serve, stir the mascarpone into the cheese
   mixture, add the kirsch to taste and enough boiling water
   to make a loose, smooth sauce. Serve with the pieces of
   chargrilled bread for dipping.

   Note: You might want to also offer other things for
   dipping, such as prawns or broccoli.

Nanny's Christmas pudding

'For many Australians, Christmas wouldn't be Christmas without a pudding! And although it's possible to make a pudding on Christmas Eve, many foodies agree November is the ideal time to make one and then store it for the big day, as puddings taste better the longer they age.' Beverley Quigley

SERVES: 8–10

375 g seeded raisins, chopped

375 g sultanas

250 g currants

185 g prunes, chopped

185 g mixed peel, chopped

finely grated zest of 1 lemon

90 g blanched almonds, chopped

1 large carrot, coarsely grated

4¼ cups soft white breadcrumbs

1 cup caster sugar

1 cup plain flour

½ teaspoon salt

½ teaspoon nutmeg

1 teaspoon mixed spice

4 eggs

¾ cup milk

½ cup brandy

½ cup stout

250 g unsalted butter, melted

1. Grease two 1 litre pudding basins (or one 2-litre basin).

2. In a large bowl, combine the raisins, sultanas, currants, prunes, mixed peel, lemon zest, almonds, carrot, breadcrumbs and sugar.

3. Sift the flour into the fruit mixture and add the salt, nutmeg and mixed spice. Stir to combine.

4. In another bowl, lightly beat the eggs and then slowly beat in the milk, brandy, stout and melted butter. Add to the fruit mixture and stir well.

5. Fill the prepared basin/s, leaving about 1 cm of room at the top.

6. Cut a round of both baking paper and foil and place over the top of the basin/s.

7. Use some string and tie it around the basin/s — make sure you leave a large loop at the top once you've tied it up so you can easily pull the string to take the basin in and out of the boiling water.

8. Place an old plate in the bottom of a large saucepan half-filled with boiling water. Carefully place the pudding basin in the pan. Make sure the water only comes two-thirds of the way up the side of the basin.

9. Place the lid on the pan and gently boil for 5 hours for the large pudding or 3 hours for two smaller ones. As the water evaporates, top it up with more boiling water.

10. On the day that the pudding is due to be served, boil for a further 2 hours before serving.

Note: Puddings keep very well in a cool cupboard or, in warmer climates, the bottom of the fridge. Just be sure to keep them in clean and dry airtight containers.

Brandy cream

'To be used with Christmas pudding as well as other puddings, this recipe has been passed down from Gertrude Hughes to daughter Phyllis Jones, to daughter-in-law Marion Jones, then great granddaughters-in-law, Michelle, another Michelle, Effie and Tracy Jones and then to great-granddaughter Kaitlynn Tremethick.' Marion Jones

SERVES: 10–14

2 eggs, separated, at room
 temperature
1½ cups caster sugar
pinch of salt

1 cup pouring cream, at room
 temperature
120 ml brandy

1. Whip the egg whites to maximum peaks while gradually adding the sugar and salt. Beat in the egg yolks and cream. Fold in the brandy.

2. Place in an airtight container which can be turned upside down if the brandy separates.

   Note: Best made the day before use.

Cornish pasties

Timeless Cornish pasties are delicious at the best of times, but when they're fresh out of your own oven and topped with a generous dollop of homemade sauce, they're delightful.

MAKES: 8

350 g rump or scotch fillet
   steak, diced
1 turnip, diced
1 carrot, diced
1 onion, chopped

4 sheets ready-rolled shortcrust
   pastry
1 egg, beaten
homemade sauce of your
   choosing, to serve

1. Preheat the oven to 180°C. Line a baking tray with baking paper.

2. Combine the steak, turnip, carrot and onion in a bowl.

3. Cut two 14 cm circles from each sheet of pastry.

4. Place ¼ cup of beef mixture in the centre of each circle. Brush the edges with water. Press the edges together to seal and form frills. Stand upright on the prepared baking tray.

5. Brush the pasties with the beaten egg. Bake for 50–60 minutes, or until golden. Serve with homemade sauce.

Fruit mince pies

MAKES: 20

750 g seeded raisins, finely chopped

125 g mixed peel, finely chopped

1 kg cooking apples, peeled and chopped

375 g currants

250 g sultanas

185 g shredded suet

½ teaspoon mixed spice

4 tablespoons lemon juice

finely grated zest of 2 lemons

3 cups caster sugar

120 ml dark rum, brandy or sherry

1 egg white

sugar, for dusting

Pastry

4 cups self-raising flour

250 g unsalted butter

¾ cup milk

1 egg yolk

1. Place the raisins, peel, apple, currants, sultanas, suet and mixed spice in a large bowl (I melt the suet in the microwave and pour it over the mixture). Add the lemon juice, zest, caster sugar and alcohol. Mix thoroughly and leave to stand overnight.

2. To make the pastry, mix the flour and butter in a food processor. While still processing, add ½ cup of milk and the egg yolk. If the mixture is too dry, add the remaining milk.

3. Turn the pastry out onto a clean work surface. Shape into a disc. Wrap the pastry in plastic wrap and refrigerate for 1 hour.

The Way Mum Made It

4. Preheat the oven to 180°C. Roll out the pastry on a lightly floured surface until 5 mm thick. Use an 8.5 cm diameter round pastry cutter to cut out 20 discs from the pastry.

5. Use a 5 cm diameter star-shaped pastry cutter to cut 20 stars from the remaining pastry.

6. Grease 20 muffin holes. Line the muffin holes with the pastry discs. Divide the fruit mince among the pastry cases. Top each with a pastry star. Brush the stars lightly with the egg white and sprinkle with the sugar.

7. Bake for 20–25 minutes, or until light golden. Set aside for 5 minutes to cool before transferring to a wire rack to cool completely.

Note 1: If the tops are overbrowning, cover with some foil.

Note 2: You can put the fruit filling into sealed containers in the fridge for a couple of months, or even freeze it if you wish.

Honey and ginger chicken wings

Always a popular appetiser to serve at a barbecue or dinner party,
these chicken wings are so simple to make and are sure to be a hit.

SERVES: 2

½ cup honey

2 teaspoons sesame oil

2 tablespoons soy sauce

3 cm piece fresh ginger, peeled
and finely grated

1 long red chilli, finely diced
(optional)

500 g chicken wings

your favourite dipping sauce,
to serve

1. Combine the honey, sesame oil, soy sauce, ginger and chilli
   (if you want an extra kick) in a glass bowl.

2. Add the chicken wings and toss to coat well. Refrigerate for
   1 hour to marinate.

3. Preheat the oven to 200 °C. Line a large baking tray with
   baking paper. Spread the chicken wings on the tray and
   roast for 25 minutes, or until golden. Serve warm with your
   favourite dipping sauce.

Strawberry trifle

"'Only for when we have guests," my mother would say. And then of course "the guests" would ask for the trifle. It's just delicious!' Rhonda Hewitt

SERVES: 6

2 x 225 g packets jam sponge
rolls
100 g packet coconut
macaroons
250 g punnet strawberries,
hulled and sliced

2 tablespoons brandy
4 eggs
2 tablespoons sugar
I cup milk
I cup pouring cream

1. Cut the jam sponge rolls into 2.5 cm thick slices. Crush the macaroons slightly.

2. In a 20 cm soufflé dish, alternate layers of cake, macaroon and strawberries.

3. In a bowl, combine the brandy, eggs, sugar, milk and cream. Pour the mixture over the trifle and stand for 30 minutes. Preheat the oven to 180°C.

4. Bake for 45 minutes, or until set.

Note: An easy and delicious dessert, especially for winter nights.

Cheesy baked artichoke dip

Rosie Kennett

MAKES: 2 ½ CUPS

½ cup grated parmesan cheese, plus 2 tablespoons extra

¼ cup mayonnaise

¼ cup sour cream

½ teaspoon pepper

½ teaspoon onion salt

½ teaspoon garlic powder

pinch of salt

60 g artichoke hearts in water, well drained, chopped into quarters

I cup grated Italian cheese blend

¼ teaspoon sweet paprika

I baguette, sliced, toasted, to serve

1. Whisk ½ cup of the grated parmesan cheese, the mayonnaise, sour cream, pepper, onion salt, garlic powder and salt in a large bowl until combined.

2. Stir in the chopped artichoke hearts. Transfer the mixture to a 3 cup ramekin.

3. Sprinkle the dip with the extra 2 tablespoons of grated parmesan cheese, the Italian cheese and paprika.

4. Preheat the oven to 190°C. Bake for 25–35 minutes, or until heated through.

5. Preheat an oven grill. Grill until the cheese melts. Serve warm with toasted baguette slices.

Curried meatballs

These bite-sized delicacies pack a powerful burst of flavour in every mouthful. Perfect for parties and sit-down dinners alike.

SERVES: 4

500 g beef mince
1 egg, lightly beaten
2 garlic cloves, crushed
¼ cup korma curry paste
2 spring onions, thinly sliced

1 x 400 g tin lentils, drained
  and rinsed
salt and pepper, to season
2 tablespoons rice bran oil
your choice of sauce, for
  dipping

1. Combine the mince, egg, garlic, curry paste, onion and lentils in a bowl. Season with salt and pepper. Mix to combine.

2. Roll level tablespoons of the mixture into balls. Place on a plate.

3. Heat the oil in a large frying pan over medium–high heat. Cook the meatballs, turning, for 5–7 minutes, or until cooked through.

4. Serve with a selection of sauces such as chutney, tomato and sweet chilli.

Marzipan hearts

'This is my late grandmother's recipe. She used to make them all the time. Especially around Christmas time. You can find marzipan everywhere in Germany. It's easy and delicious. Making these reminds me of her.' Gisela Engelhardt

MAKES: 18–24

Marzipan
300 g ground almonds
250 g icing sugar, sifted
2 tablespoons rosewater
Hearts
1 egg

200 g icing sugar, sifted
Filling
1 egg white
150 g icing sugar, sifted
½ teaspoon lemon juice

1. To make the raw marzipan, mix the ground almonds and icing sugar together in a food processor until there are no lumps. Add the rosewater and knead the dough until a thick, elastic mass is formed. To store the dough, form a log, wrap it in plastic wrap and refrigerate. (The raw dough lasts about a month in the fridge and six months in the freezer.)

2. To make the hearts, separate the egg yolk from the egg white (set the egg white aside) and knead it and the sifted icing sugar with the raw marzipan.

3. Roll out half of the dough and cut out little hearts. From the rest of the dough, cut some long thin strips and brush the top with the lightly whipped egg white. Wrap the strips around the edge of the hearts and press on firmly. To make a nice pattern, press a few notches with a needle into the border and brush it with the egg white.

4. Preheat the oven to 200°C. Place the hearts on a baking tray lined with baking paper. Bake until the borders start to turn golden brown.

5. To make the filling, mix the egg white, sifted icing sugar and lemon juice and fill the centre of the hearts.

   Note 1: If the dough is too dry to knead, you can put 1 tablespoon of vegetable oil or almond oil into the mix.

   Note 2: For extra delicious pralines, instead of making the hearts you can also roll your raw marzipan in liquid chocolate and let it dry. You can also use it as fondant for cakes.

Toby's homemade chicken sandwiches

SERVES: 5

400 g chicken, cooked
½ cup toasted pine nuts
½ cup chopped parsley
¾ cup whole-egg mayonnaise
¼ cup sour cream

salt and pepper, to season
⅓ cup chopped chives
½ cup chopped celery
10 slices bread

1. Place all of the ingredients, except the bread, in a food processor and blend until well combined.

2. Spread one slice of bread with the filling and top with another piece of bread. Repeat until five sandwiches are made.

Hot cross buns

*Nothing says Easter like a batch of hot cross buns fresh out of the oven.
Simply add butter and a cup of tea and you'll be in foodie heaven.*

MAKES: 12

1 tablespoon dried yeast
1 teaspoon caster sugar, plus
   ⅓ cup, plus 2 tablespoons
   extra for glaze
¾ cup warm milk
½ cup cold milk
50 g unsalted butter, melted,
   plus extra for greasing

1 egg, lightly whisked
3½ cups plain flour, plus
   ½ cup extra for crosses
200 g mixed dried fruit
2 teaspoons mixed spice
pinch of salt
½ cup plain flour
2 tablespoons caster sugar

1. To make the dough, mix the yeast, 1 teaspoon of sugar and
   the warm milk in a jug. Set aside for 10 minutes, or until
   frothy. Whisk in the cold milk, the melted butter and the
   egg.

2. Combine the flour, dried fruit, ⅓ cup of sugar, mixed spice
   and salt in a bowl. Make a well in the centre. Add the yeast
   mixture. Use a wooden spoon to stir until combined, then
   use your hands to bring the dough together in the bowl.

3. Turn out onto a lightly floured surface and knead for
   10–15 minutes, or until smooth and elastic. Place in a
   greased bowl. Cover with plastic wrap. Set aside for 1 hour
   30 minutes, or until doubled in size.

4. To shape the buns, punch down the centre of the dough with your fist. Knead on a lightly floured surface for 2 minutes. Shape into 12 even portions.

5. Brush a tin with melted butter to grease. Place the portions side by side in the prepared tin. Cover with a clean tea towel. Set aside in a warm, draught-free place to prove for 30 minutes, or until doubled in size.

6. Preheat the oven to 200°C.

7. Combine ½ cup of flour with a little water to make a paste. Place in a sealable plastic bag. Cut one corner from the bag to make a 2 mm hole. Pipe crosses onto the buns.

8. Bake for 10 minutes. Reduce the oven temperature to 160°C. Bake for 20 minutes, or until golden and cooked through.

9. Meanwhile, place 2 tablespoons of sugar and ⅔ cup of water in a saucepan over low heat and cook until the sugar dissolves. Simmer until the glaze thickens. Transfer the buns to a wire rack. Brush the tops with the glaze. Set aside to cool slightly or serve with butter when desired.

Ginger chicken meatballs

*Equally perfect for parties and dinner fare, these ginger chicken
meatballs pack a mouthful of flavour in every bite.*

SERVES: 6

400 g chicken mince
1 egg, lightly beaten
1 cup cooked long-grain rice
1 cup fresh breadcrumbs
2 garlic cloves, crushed
½ cup finely chopped
   coriander leaves

2 spring onions, thinly sliced
3 cm piece fresh ginger, finely
   grated
½ cup sweet chilli sauce
salt and pepper, to season
2 tablespoons peanut oil

1. Combine the mince, egg, rice, breadcrumbs, garlic,
   coriander, spring onion, ginger and 2 tablespoons of sweet
   chilli sauce in a bowl. Season with salt and pepper. Mix to
   combine.

2. Roll the mixture into even-sized balls. Set aside on a plate.

3. Heat the oil in a large frying pan over medium–high heat.
   Cook the meatballs, turning, for 5–7 minutes, or until
   browned and cooked through.

4. Serve with the remaining sweet chilli sauce (or soy sauce)
   and an accompaniment of your choosing — salad or noodles
   work best.

Mini smoked salmon and parsley quiches

Whether you're entertaining guests or want to make something a little different for the grandkids, these salmon mini quiches are easy to make, not to mention delicious.

MAKES: 12

1 packet filo pastry or 3 sheets
   frozen puff pastry, thawed
100 g sliced smoked salmon,
   chopped
2 tablespoons chopped parsley

2 tablespoons chopped chives
1½ tablespoons spreadable
   cream cheese
2 eggs
⅔ cup pouring cream

1. Preheat the oven to 190°C. Lightly grease two 12-hole patty cake tins.

2. Use a 7 cm cutter to cut rounds from the pastry and line the tins with the pastry rounds.

3. Divide the salmon, herbs and cream cheese evenly between the pastry shells.

4. Whisk the eggs and cream together and carefully pour into the shells.

5. Bake for 20 minutes, or until puffed and golden brown (they will sink on cooling). Lift the quiches from the tins and place on a wire rack to cool.

The Way Mum Made It

Sauces, preserves and jams

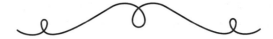

'Cooking is hard work, but when it is done with love,
it really is a pleasure.'
— Margaret Fulton

Cooking doesn't have to end with preparing a meal —
why not try bottling your own sauces, jams or preserves?
As well as showing your guests how talented you are, a
homemade bottled condiment makes a lovely and very
thoughtful gift.

How to sterilise jars and bottles

In order to prevent contamination — and thus lengthen the shelf life — of your sauces, preserves and jams it's extremely important to sterilise your jars or bottles before storing your homemade goodies. Follow our step-by-step guide here.

1. Preheat the oven to 110°C. Wash the jars and lids in hot, soapy water. Rinse well. Place the jars and lids in a deep saucepan. Cover with cold water.

2. Bring the water to the boil over high heat. Cover the pan. Reduce the heat to medium and boil gently for 10 minutes. Line a baking tray with a clean tea towel.

3. Using metal tongs, remove the jars and lids from the boiling water and place upside down on the tray. Place in the oven and heat for 15 minutes.

4. Now you're ready to bottle your goodies. Just remember: place hot sauces, preserves or jams in hot jars and cooled sauces, preserves or jams in cold jars.

Curry sauce

'I have been using this sauce since the '60s. Originally I used it for curried eggs but it also works well for fish, tinned or fresh, chopped leftover roast meat, or vegetables, like pumpkin when the garden is overflowing!' Kate Huston

MAKES: 1½ CUPS

1 tablespoon butter
1 onion, finely chopped
1 granny smith apple, grated
1 tablespoon curry powder or
  paste
1 teaspoon crushed garlic

1 tablespoon tomato paste
1 tablespoon plain flour
salt and pepper, to season
1 cup chicken stock
juice of ½ lemon

1. Melt the butter in a saucepan over medium heat. Add the onion and apple and gently sauté, stirring constantly.

2. Stir in the curry powder or paste, garlic, tomato paste, flour and salt and pepper and cook for 2 minutes. Slowly stir in the stock and simmer for about 5 minutes, stirring occasionally. Taste for seasoning.

Note: This sauce can be kept in an airtight container in the freezer for up to 4 months.

Variations: For egg curry, add boiled eggs, cut lengthways. You can stir 1 chopped egg into the sauce.

For salmon curry, add chunks of tinned pink salmon.

For vegetable curry, add cooked chunks of potato, pumpkin or sweet potato — all work well.

Plum jam

*'This was my mother's recipe. It's good, old, plain
and simple but the tastiest jam.' Judy Coburn*

MAKES: 6 X 500 G JARS

900 g plums, halved and
   stoned
¼ teaspoon salt

450 g sugar
1 tablespoon lemon juice

1. Place the plums in a saucepan, add 3 tablespoons of water
    and the salt and bring to the boil over medium heat. Simmer
    for 10 minutes.

2. Add the sugar and lemon juice and bring to the boil.
    Continue boiling until the mixture reaches setting point.
    To test, place a small amount of the mixture in a saucer. If it
    sets, it's ready.

3. Cool the mixture for 15 minutes, then spoon into warm
    sterilised jars and seal while hot.

Healthy tomato sauce

*From grandkids to grandparents, tomato sauce is
definitely a favourite come dinnertime. Why not make
your own healthy version? It's super-simple.*

MAKES: 4 x 500 ML BOTTLES

1 tablespoon olive oil
2 onions, roughly chopped
1 tablespoon salt
pinch of pepper
7–8 x 400 g tins crushed or
  diced tomatoes
2 red capsicums, roughly
  chopped
4 garlic cloves
1 celery stalk, roughly chopped

½ cup raw or soft brown sugar
½ teaspoon cayenne pepper
  (optional)
1 tablespoon sweet paprika
  (optional)
6 whole cloves (optional)
1 cinnamon stick (optional)
1½ cups red or white wine
  vinegar

1. Heat the oil in a large saucepan over medium heat. Add the
   onion and cook, stirring occasionally, until soft but not
   caramelised. Add the salt and season well with the pepper.

2. Add the tomatoes, capsicum, garlic and celery to the pan
   and increase the heat to medium–high. Cook, stirring, until
   the tomatoes have broken down and the vegetables are soft.
   Remove from the heat and allow the mixture to cool slightly.

3. Pour the mixture into a food processor and process until partially puréed. Strain the mixture through a sieve into a jug to remove the seeds and tomato skin. Return to the food processor and process until finely puréed.

4. Return the mixture to the saucepan over medium–low heat. Add the sugar and the cayenne pepper, paprika, cloves and cinnamon stick (if using). Cook, stirring occasionally, for 30 minutes, or until the sauce thickens.

5. Add the vinegar and continue cooking until the mixture is slightly runnier than your desired result, as it will thicken as it cools. Remove the cinnamon stick, if necessary. Taste and season with salt and pepper.

6. Remove from the heat and set aside to cool slightly. Transfer the mixture to a heatproof jug.

7. Prepare four sterilised glass bottles with screw-cap lids and, using a funnel, pour the sauce into the bottles. Allow the sauce to cool in the bottle, then seal tightly with the screw-cap lid and label with the date.

Note: You can store the sauce, unopened, for up to 12 months. After opening, store in the fridge for up to 12 weeks.

Watermelon jam

MAKES: 10 X 250 ML JARS

4 cups caster sugar
8 cups watermelon, rind and
  seeds removed

1–2 x 50 g sachets of Jamsetta
juice of 2 lemons

1. Add the sugar to a saucepan over low heat and heat until
    warm.

2. Purée the watermelon in batches using a stick blender.

3. Add the watermelon and 1 cup of water to a large saucepan
    over medium heat and bring to the boil.

4. Add the Jamsetta, lemon juice and warmed sugar and
    bring back to the boil for 15-20 minutes, stirring often and
    skimming the scum from the surface with a slotted spoon.
    Add more water if necessary.

5. Test to see if the jam is set by removing the pan from the
    heat and skimming a small amount of jam onto the end of a
    wooden spoon. After 40 seconds, if the jam crinkles when
    you run a teaspoon through it, it is set. If not, cook for a
    further 3 minutes, then repeat.

6. If your jam isn't setting, add an extra 25 g of Jamsetta, boil
    for a further 5 minutes and repeat.

7. Ladle the hot jam into warm sterilised jam jars until three-quarters full. Seal with the covers that come with Jamsetta sachets.

Note: Don't leave the saucepan unattended. It can take a while to heat up and then boil quite suddenly.

Tomato relish

Marje Hall

MAKES: 6 x 250 ML JARS

2.7 kg tomatoes
900 g onions
1 handful salt
475 ml brown malt vinegar

900 g sugar
2 tablespoons curry powder
3 teaspoons cayenne pepper

1. Pour boiling water over the tomatoes. Roughly chop the
    tomatoes and onions. Cover with salt and leave overnight.
    Drain well.

2. Add the vinegar to a saucepan over medium heat and cook
    for 5 minutes. Add the sugar and spices. Add the tomato
    mixture. Boil for 1–1½ hours. Allow to cool slightly.

3. Spoon the relish into warm sterilised glass jars. Allow the
    relish to cool in the jars, then seal tightly with screw-cap lids
    and label with the date.

    Note: The relish will keep unopened in a cool, dry
    pantry for up to 1 year.

Lemon butter

*It's not often that people think to add condiments other than
cream to baked goods, but we're on a mission to change that.
This lemon butter is wonderful on toast, muffins, scones,
gingerbread or walnut loaf. It also makes a thoughtful gift
for family and friends. And it's so simple to make.*

MAKES: 2 X 250 ML JARS

4 large eggs
¾ cup sugar
½ cup lemon juice

2 teaspoons lemon zest
125 g unsalted butter, chopped

1. Set a heatproof bowl over a pot of gently simmering water.
    Add the eggs and sugar to the bowl and whisk constantly
    until the sugar has dissolved.

2. Add the juice, lemon zest and butter. Continue to whisk for
    a further 20 minutes, or until the mixture is smooth and
    is thick enough to coat your spoon. Do not let the mixture
    boil.

3. Pour the warm mixture into hot sterilised jars and seal
    immediately.

    Note: Lemon butter will keep in the fridge for up to 1
    month.

Three-ingredient pasta sauce

The supermarket offers a dizzying array of pasta sauce options. But once you discover just how easy it is to make yourself, you'll never need to purchase it again. Next time you visit your local fruit shop or market, keep an eye out for the super-cheap, overripe tomatoes. These are perfect for your sauce, and easy on your wallet.

MAKES: 8 CUPS

2 kg fresh, ripe tomatoes

3 onions, quartered

3 tablespoons olive oil

1. Preheat the oven to 180°C. Slice each tomato in half and place on a baking tray.

2. Sprinkle the onion over the tomato. Cover the tomato and onion in the oil and use your hands to massage it in.

3. Bake in the oven for about 1 hour, or until the tomato is tender and juicy.

4. Allow to cool slightly, then place in a food processor to blend until smooth.

5. Allow to cool completely before storing in the freezer for up to 6 months.

Note 1: Tasty ideas that you could add before puréeing:

2 finely chopped red chillies	½ cup red wine
1 handful basil	2 cups roasted red capsicum
1 cup cooked and chopped	(cook with the tomatoes)
mushrooms	

Note 2: Once prepared, you can easily store the sauce in the freezer. Freeze in ice-cube trays or measure out 1 cup portions to freeze in containers or zip-lock bags. You can then thaw overnight in the fridge or in the microwave as needed.

Strawberry jam

Rosie Kennett

MAKES: 3 X 125 ML JARS

450 g strawberries
680 g caster sugar

1 teaspoon tartaric acid

1. Mash the strawberries. Add to a saucepan over low heat and slowly bring to the boil for 5 minutes.

2. Add the sugar, stirring constantly, and bring to the boil for 1 minute.

3. Add the tartaric acid and boil for a further 4 minutes. (Do not boil for more than 8 minutes altogether.)

4. Stir to cool and also to make sure the strawberries won't rise to the top. Spoon into warm sterilised jars and seal.

   Note: This jam can be stored in the fridge for up to 1 month.

Mint sauce

*This classic English mint sauce is so easy to make
you'll never buy store-bought versions again!*

SERVES: 6

1 large bunch mint, finely
  chopped
2 teaspoons caster sugar

4 tablespoons boiling water
4 tablespoons white wine
  vinegar

1. Combine the mint and caster sugar in a heatproof bowl.

2. Add the boiling water and stir until the sugar dissolves. Set
   aside to cool.

3. Stir in the vinegar and mix well. Taste, then add more water
   or vinegar as desired.

4. Spoon into warm sterilised glass jars. Seal tightly with
   screw-cap lids.

   Note: This sauce can be stored in the fridge for up to 1
   week.

Grapefruit and orange marmalade

*'This originally came from a 1975 Nursing Mothers'
Association Cookbook and was given to me by my sister-in-
law (Margie Mumford) who was a midwife. I have adapted
it slightly by cutting down the sugar.' Susan Hunt*

MAKES: 12 X 250 ML JARS

1 kg grapefruit or oranges   2.5 kg caster sugar
2 lemons

1. Juice the fruit, reserving the pips. Place the pips in a muslin
    bag.

2. Chop the fruit roughly and process in a food processor.
    Place the fruit, juice, muslin bag and 2.5 litres of water in a
    pan and soak overnight.

3. Bring the pan to the boil and simmer gently for 45 minutes,
    or until the fruit is soft.

4. Add the sugar to a saucepan over low heat and heat until
    warm.

5. Add the warmed sugar to the fruit mixture and stir until
    dissolved. Boil the mixture rapidly for 45 minutes, or until
    the setting point is reached, skimming occasionally. Cool
    for a few minutes.

6. Pour the mixture into sterilised jars and seal with the lids.

   Note 1: Over the years I have made this with just grapefruit or a combination of grapefruit and oranges. Now that we have our own navel orange tree, I make it with just our oranges but always with the lemons.

   Note 2: The marmalade can be stored unopened in a cool, dark place for up to 12 months. Once opened, store in the fridge for up to 6 weeks.

Index

A

almonds
  Filomena's health bread, 54–5
  Gluten-free orange cake, 115–16
  Lemon and butter almond slice, 96–7
  Marzipan hearts, 246–7
Anzac biscuits, 233–4
Apple and caramel upside-down cake, 93–4
Apple and cinnamon teacake, 87–8
Apple fritters, 19–20
Apple pie, 79–81
Apple turnovers, 72–3
apples
  Apple and caramel upside-down cake, 93–4
  Apple and cinnamon teacake, 87–8
  Apple fritters, 18
  Apple pie, 79–81
  Apple turnovers, 72–3
  Baked sticky date apples, 33–4
  Fruit mince pies, 240–1
  Lumberjack cake, 70–1
  Toffee apples, 126
Apricot bran loaf, 16
Apricot chicken, 194
Apricot loaf, 74
apricots
  Apricot bran loaf, 16
  Apricot chicken, 194
  Apricot loaf, 74
  Coconut and apricot cake, 98
artichokes
  Cheesy baked artichoke dip, 244
Asparagus ribbon tart, 47

B

bacon
  Bubble-and-squeak croquettes, 199–200
  Chicken, bacon and pumpkin pasta bake, 170–1
  Classic club sandwich, 156
  Fresh pea, mint and bacon salad, 157
  Lambs fry and bacon, 201–2
  Last-minute carbonara, 143
  Quiche Lorraine, 176–7
  Zucchini slice, 18
Baked eggplant, 189–90
Baked fish fingers, 114
Baked rice custard, 58
Baked sticky date apples, 33–4
Banana and walnut overnight oats, 17
Banana bread, 77–8
Banana pikelets, 14
Banana split toasted sandwich, 137
bananas
  Banana and walnut overnight oats, 17
  Banana bread, 77–8
  Banana pikelets, 14
  Banana split toasted sandwich, 137
  Healthy banana and walnut muffins, 29–30
  Raspberry banana bread with passionfruit icing, 41–2
barbecue
  Chicken satay skewers, 228–9
  Jerk chicken drumsticks, 221
beans See lentils and beans
Bechamel (Classic moussaka), 206–7
Bechamel (Lasagne), 184

Curried meatballs, 245
Curry sauce, 255–6

D
dates
    Baked sticky date apples, 33–4
    Lumberjack cake, 70–1
    Rock cakes, 61
    Steamed date pudding, 86
Delicious salmon spread, 15
desserts
    Apple turnovers, 72–3
    Baked rice custard, 58
    Baked sticky date apples, 33–4
    Cream cheese slice, 63
    Tiramisu, 219–20
    Vanilla custard squares, 82
    See also cakes; cupcakes; slices (sweet);
        teacakes; tortes; treats
dips *See* spreads and dips (savoury)
dressings
    Niçoise salad, 164
    Tangy coleslaw, 155
    Three-bean salad, 160
drinks
    Extra sour lemon ice tea, 28
    Kiwifruit and rockmelon smoothie,
        39
    Lemon cordial, 105
    Prawn cocktails, 211
    Rhubarb champagne, 224
    Sparkling punch, 210
Dutch honey cake, 90

E
Easy fruitcake, 67–8
Easy lentil stew, 193
eggplants
    Baked eggplant, 189–90
    Classic moussaka, 206–7
eggs
    Apple and caramel upside-down
        cake, 93–4
    Asparagus ribbon tart, 47
    Broccoli quiche, 43–4
    Chocolate coconut meringue torte,
        64–5
    Gluten-free orange cake, 115–16
    Grandma's never-fail sponge cake,
        59–60

Kill me quicks, 227
Lemon and butter almond slice, 96–7
Lemon butter, 263
Noodle omelette, 152
Pavlova, 215–16
Quiche Lorraine, 176–7
Simple baked eggs in chunky tomato
    sauce, 22
Zucchini slice, 18
Extra sour lemon ice tea, 28

F
fennel, Potato and fennel tarte tatin,
    31–2
Filomena's health bread, 54–5
fish *See* cod; salmon; tuna
Fish pie, 110–11
Five-cup loaf, 21
Fluffy blueberry pancakes, 36
Frankfurts, tomato and onion, 183
Fresh pea, mint and bacon salad, 157
fritters
    Apple fritters, 19–20
    Corn fritters, 25
Fruit mince pies, 240–1
Fudge, 66

G
garlic
    Easy garlic bread, 125
    Garlic and herb pull-apart bread,
        37–8
    Roast leg of lamb with 50 cloves of
        garlic, 180
Garlic and herb pull-apart bread, 37–8
Garlic and parmesan roasted pumpkin,
    232
Gin and tonic cupcakes, 84–5
Ginger chicken meatballs, 251
Gluten-free
    Baked rice custard, 58
    Baked sticky date apples, 33
    Beetroot hummus, 133
    Brandy cream, 238
    Brown rice, lentil and feta salad, 145
    Cheesy potato bake, 225–6
    Chocolate coconut meringue torte,
        64–5
    Clam chowder, 181–2
    Cobb salad, 150

 Alexandra O'Brien's love of cooking was inspired by her late grandmother, Patricia Smith, with whom Alex spent much time in the kitchen when she was a little girl. Pat was not only an amazing cook who taught her own three daughters, as well as Alexandra and her four sisters, the pleasure of home-style cooking, but she also imbued in each of them the know-how to hold events, having honed everything from the menu planning, cooking and hosting down to a fine art. Bringing loved ones together over a meal — from afternoon teas and weekly dinners to special occasions and holidays — became a family tradition.

As the editor of Over60, Alex's passion for cooking has evolved into unearthing recipes from the Over60 community each day. Sharing cherished family recipes that have been passed down for generations, Over60 are not just renowned for the community-contributed recipes, but are loved because the community get a chance to tell the beautiful stories behind them.